MW00560865

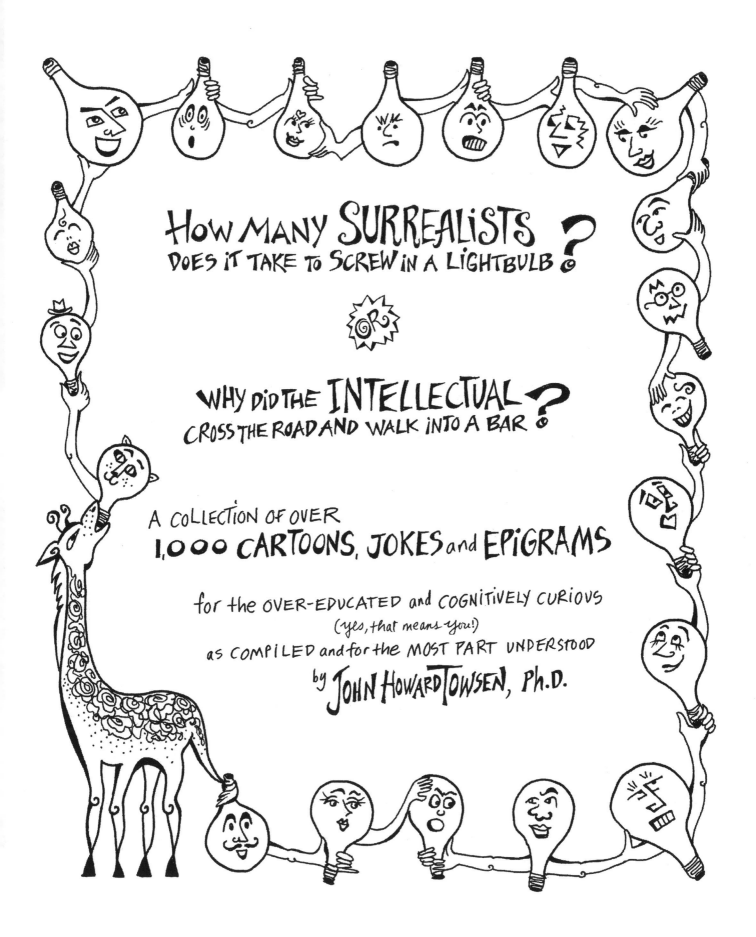

HOW MANY SURREALISTS ?
DOES IT TAKE TO SCREW IN A LIGHTBULB ?

OR

WHY DID THE INTELLECTUAL ?
CROSS THE ROAD AND WALK INTO A BAR ?

A COLLECTION OF OVER
1,000 CARTOONS, JOKES and EPIGRAMS

for the OVER-EDUCATED and COGNITIVELY CURIOUS
(yes, that means you!)
as COMPILED and for the MOST PART UNDERSTOOD
by JOHN HOWARD TOWSEN, Ph.D.

Cover design by Flash Rosenberg
Book layout by John Towsen

First published: 2015

NY: Arlecchino Books.

© John Towsen

ISBN-13: 978-0692488560

All rights reserved. No part of this publication may
be reproduced, distributed, or transmitted in any
form or by any means, including photocopying,
recording, or other electronic or mechanical
methods, without the prior written permission of
the publisher, except in the case of brief quotations
embodied in critical reviews and certain other
noncommercial uses permitted by copyright law.
Copyright information for individual cartoons can
be found in the *Cartoonist Index* at the back of the
book.

www.ArlecchinoBooks.com.

Printed in the United States of America

Preface or Foreword
(I'm Not Sure Which)

I had the idea for this book in the late 80s, and it almost made it into print in 1992. But despite a top-notch agent and some real interest by editors at major houses (including Jackie Kennedy at Doubleday) it turned out nobody wanted to pay so many cartoonists for so many cartoons. Other priorities —and this thing called life— took over and so this particular project went on the back burner for 2+ decades. Last year, aided by more free time, some money I could call my own, but no increase in common sense, I returned to the scene of the crime and solved this dilemma by paying the cartoonists myself. Some of my favorite cartoonists (e.g., Gary Larson, Zach Weiner, XKCD, Hap Kliban) were unavailable for licensing, but I got pretty much everyone else whose work fit the book content. Some had sent me work in 1992 and were quite surprised to find me contacting them again 23 years later, checkbook in hand. Patience is indeed a virtue.

The jokes are from everywhere, the result of a quarter century of collecting but —for better or for worse— their final wording is mine, as is the layout of the book.

As you flip through these pages it will become obvious that this collection of "intellectual" humor is in no way an intellectual analysis of humor. I enjoy experiencing comedy and I enjoy creating comedy, but my brain freezes over when it comes to analyzing how humor works. You might as well try telling me your dreams. As E.B. White said, "Analyzing humor is like dissecting a frog. Few people are interested and the frog dies of it." I do, however, choose to believe that the humor in these pages is both entertaining *and* enlightening, and will be of the longer-lasting, thought-provoking variety. In fact, that's pretty much the point of the whole book.

I should confess that quote attribution in this book may not always be historically accurate. Clever epigrams tend to get attributed to celebrities, not to their writers, and even less

so to the anonymous soul who may have first turned a similar phrase. As the late, great Yogi Berra said, "I never said most of the things I said."

In my physical comedy blog, I often enjoy tracing gags back in time, but in this book, which is after all for entertainment purposes, I have been content to let famous people take credit for the wittiness attributed to them. Lynne Fontane was not the first to say "divorce, never; murder, many times," but it sure fits her life story and, let's face it, sounds funnier than if I told you it predates her by fifty years, which it probably does. For those of you who are stricter about these matters, web sites such as *quoteinvestigator.com* and *snopes.com* should prove useful.

I would also add that you probably won't get every joke in the book. I know I didn't, but that's okay. Since I'm not out to explain humor, you're on your own, but you can always look them up... or write me a letter. But I will tell you this, since you deserve some kind of reward for bothering to read this page: the review of *Lady Chatterly's Lover* on page 139 did indeed appear in *Field & Stream*, but was in fact written as a spoof. Now aren't you glad you read the preface or the foreword, instead of remaining forever curious about that one?

I'm excited to imagine lots of folks smiling and laughing their way through this book and the work of all these brilliant humorists. I'll be even more excited if they buy copies for everyone on their holiday/birthday/graduation gift list — and by *they* I mean *you*. Also, please don't *you* forget to review it (favorably) for a major national publication. Or at the very least say something nice about it on Amazon. Finally, let me urge you to buy work by these cartoonists (see *Cartoonist Index* at the back of the book). Keep creative people creating!

Meanwhile, enjoy...

John Towsen
New York City
October 2015

This book is dedicated to ALL my laugh mates —some sadly no longer with us— kindred spirits whose friendship and sense of humor have kept me going for the past half century, especially Susan Avino, Hovey Burgess, Linnea Conway, Rick Davis, Val Dean, Angela Delfini, Marshall Dodge, Jango Edwards, Avner Eisenberg, Ken Feit, Judy Finelli, Karen Flaherty, Mona Friedman, Karen Gersch, Diane L. Goodman, Yael Goverover, Jan Greenfield, Judith Harding, Jessica Hentoff, Deborah Kauffman, Riley Kellogg, Joe Killian, John Krol, Martie LaBare, Fred Lown, Carlo Mazzone-Clementi, Michael McGuigan, Jim Moore, Theresa Mori, Zeke Peterhoff, Richard Pochinko, Lisa Rabinowitz, Drew Richardson, Don Rieder, Noel Selegzi, Mike Seliger, Rhona Sewell, Joanna Sherman, Hank Smith, Jesse Towsen, Nathaniel Towsen, Aaron Watkins, Mary Wise, Fred Yockers, and Michael Zerphy. Yes, in alphabetical order because you know how competitive funny people can get!

Special Thanks

This project would not have gotten very far off the back burner without the diligent and much appreciated assistance of both my copyright specialist, Sandy Schechter, and my sweetheart and partner, Riley Kellogg, whose eye for text and visuals proved invaluable. Further thanks are due to a team of friends whose feedback on many of the cartoons and jokes forced me to think twice about what was funny and who my audience is: Shane Baker, Mona Friedman, Pat Judd, Riley Kellogg (again!), Martha LaBare, Ted Lawrence, Lisa Rabinowitz, Noel Selegzi, Mike Seliger, Rhona Sewell, Richard Steifel, Jesse Towsen, Nathaniel Towsen, and Alyssa Varner. Many thanks all!

Contents

Chapter One

The Meaning of Life

or, What's in It for Me?

Kirk Anderson

"A philosopher," said the theologian, "is like a blind man in a darkened room looking for a black cat that isn't there."

"That's right," the philosopher replied, "and if he were a theologian, he'd find it."

God @TheTweetOfGod:
It's too bad the meaning of life is 141 characters long.
—David Javerbaum, *An Act of God*

God and Solomon are talking. God says, "You can have infinite beauty, infinite wealth, or infinite wisdom. What's it going to be?"

Solomon says, "Infinite wisdom."

A moment passes. Solomon slaps his forehead and says, "I shoulda taken the money!"

"There is a theory which states that if ever anyone discovers exactly what the Universe is for and why it is here, it will instantly disappear and be replaced by something even more bizarre and inexplicable.

"There is another theory which states that this has already happened."
—Douglas Adams, *The Restaurant at the End of the Universe*

An elderly woman approached the poet Samuel Taylor Coleridge after a lecture and confided, "Mr. Coleridge, I've accepted the universe." Coleridge gave her the once over, looked her straight in the eye, and said, "My God, madam, you'd better!"

Francis Acupan

The Meaning of Life

Charlie Rodrigues

"I think, therefore I am is the statement of an intellectual who underrates toothaches."
  —Milan Kundera

I think tiramisu, therefore I'm having tiramisu.
  —René Dessertcartes.

Cogito ergo spud. I think, therefore I yam.
  —graffiti by way of Herb Caen

Cogito hair-goo some. I think I need more styling gel.
  —Gore Vidal Sassoon

I can be Googled, therefore I am.

René Descartes walks into a restaurant and the waiter asks him if he'd like a menu.
Descartes says, "I think not" and — *PUFF*— he disappears.

"I think I think; therefore, I think I am."
  —Ambrose Bierce

"A gloss on Descartes: Sometimes I think, and sometimes I am."
  —Paul Valéry

WHILE SEARCHING FOR A UNIVERSAL TRUTH, PAUL FOUND HIS OTHER BLACK SOCK

Paul Soderblom

"Gee, I don't know, Mister — hey, Norm, if a tree falls in the forest and there's nobody there, is there any sound?"

Charlie Rodrigues

"If a man is talking in the forest, and there's no woman there to hear him, is he still wrong?"
—Jenny Weber

"What if everything is an illusion and nothing exists? In that case, I definitely overpaid for my carpet."
—Woody Allen

"Reality is merely an illusion, albeit a very persistent one."
—Albert Einstein

If a tree falls in the forest, do the other trees laugh at it?

If a tree falls in the forest and lands on a deaf person, how funny is that?

If a tree screams in space and no one is there to hear it, does it still fall down?

Leigh Rubin

Leo Cullum

A chicken and an egg are lying in bed. The chicken is smoking a cigarette with a satisfied smile on his face. The egg, looking considerably less pleased, mutters, "Well, I guess we answered *that* question!"

My goal is to live in a world where a chicken can cross the road without its motives being questioned.

"Yesterday I told a chicken to cross the road. It said, 'What for?'"
—Steven Wright

Why did the chicken go to the seance?
—He wanted to get to the other side.

Is it solipsistic in here, or is it just me?

I wanted to draw a cartoon about free will but I decided not to.

"Anyone informed that the universe is expanding and contracting in pulsations of eighty billion years has a right to ask, 'What's in it for me?'"
—Peter De Vries

"Once you can accept the universe as matter expanding into nothing that is something, wearing stripes with plaid comes easy."
—Albert Einstein

There are two types of people in the world: those who divide the world into two types of people, and those wise enough to know better.

THE PHYSICIST AND THE PHILOSOPHER

Doug Savage

Danny Shanahan

Graffiti on a rest room wall:
"God is dead." —Nietzsche
"Nietzsche is dead." —God

Jean-Paul Sartre is sitting at a table in the Deux Magots café in Paris, revising his draft of *Being and Nothingness*. He says to the waiter, "I'd like a cup of coffee, please, with no cream."

The waiter replies, "I'm sorry, Monsieur, but we're out of cream. Can it be with no milk?"

"To be is to do."
—Lao Tzu

"To do is to be."
—Jean Paul Sartre

"Do Be Do Be Do."
—Frank Sinatra

Andy Singer

"Exactly what is this 'nothing' I've been hearing so much about?"

David Sipress

The university president sighed as he went over the proposed budget offered him by the head of the Department of Physics.

"Why is it," he complained, "that you physicists always require so much expensive equipment? The Department of Mathematics, on the other hand, asks nothing of me but money for paper, pencils, and erasers."

He thought a while longer and added, "And the Department of Philosophy is better still. They don't even ask for erasers."

"I was thrown out of college for cheating on the metaphysics exam: I looked into the soul of another boy."
—Woody Allen

Andrew was a shy teenager about to go out on his first date. Luckily his father was a professor of philosophy and more than willing to give him some learned advice.

"Andrew," he explained, "there are three subjects that always work with women: there's food, there's family, but above all there's philosophy."

That evening Andrew met his date at a restaurant and they sat down opposite each other. After the opening pleasantries, an eternity seemed to go by without a word being spoken, making Andrew even more nervous. Suddenly remembering his father's advice, he blurted out, "Do you like Hungarian goulash?"

"No." More awkward silence.

"Do you have a brother?"

"No." Deadly silence.

Playing his last card, Andrew finally asked: "Well, if you had a brother, would he like Hungarian goulash?"

©2010 Scott Hilburn/Distributed by Universal Uclick

© 2010 Scott Hilburn. Dist. By UNIVERSAL UCLICK.
Reprinted with permission. All rights reserved.

Scott Hilburn

"There's a difference between a philosophy and a bumper sticker."
—Charles M. Schulz

Hilary Price

How do philosophy professors greet one another?
—"Hello, why are you?"

Mark Stivers

CALVIN AND HOBBES © 1991 Watterson. Reprinted with permission of UNIVERSAL UCLICK. All rights reserved.

Bill Watterson

Great questions of our time.

Graham Sale

W hat is Mind? — No Matter
What is Matter? — Never Mind

"W hat is reality, anyway? Just a
collective hunch."
—Lily Tomlin

W hat if the hokey-pokey really
is what it's all about?

"I tell you, we are here on Earth
to fart around, and don't let
anybody tell you different."
—Kurt Vonnegut

"B elieve those who seek the
truth, doubt those who
find it."
—André Gide

"T here ain't no answer.
There ain't gonna be any answer.
There never has been an answer.
There's your answer."
—Gertrude Stein

Kirk Anderson

Joe worked very hard for a very long time, assuming that if he made a lot of money and could buy anything he wanted, he would indeed be a Master of the Universe. After a decade of relentless striving, he finally succeeded in becoming rich. He realized to his dismay, however, that he just wasn't happy. There must be more to life, figured Joe, so he gave all his money away and began his Search for Meaning.

He became a drifter, wandering the world over, looking for the true meaning of life. Eventually he heard inspiring stories of a guru who lived on a Tibetan mountaintop, a spirit so evolved that he truly understood the profound essence of being human.

Joe was determined to ask the guru the meaning of life, and so set off on a quest to locate him. After weeks of a grueling trek through the densest jungle, slicing his way through the thorniest thickets and wading into the most pestilent swamps, he finally reached the base of the guru's mountaintop abode. With one final push, he scaled the steep precipice, sweating and toiling beyond belief, his skin pockmarked with cuts and bruises long before he reached the top. When he eventually got there, Joe was beyond total physical exhaustion, but somehow managed to bow down in front of the guru and ask him the meaning of life.

The guru calmly contemplated the question for a few moments, took a deep breath, and serenely replied, "Life is a bowl of cherries."

Joe said, "What!? You mean I crossed three continents, sweated blood, slogged across The Swamp from Hell, scaled a Himalayan peak, got my clothes and half my skin ripped to shreds seeking only one thing, the meaning of life, and you tell me it's a bowl of cherries?!?"

There was a long pause during which the guru's composure gave way to extreme puzzlement and then dismay. Finally he spoke: "You mean... life isn't a bowl of cherries??"

And then there was Mrs. Rothstein, who had arrived in the wilds of northern India in search of a great swami who had appeared in the foothills of the high Himalayas.

She had been warned that her trip would be a dangerous one, fraught with unimaginable perils, but she was insistent: "Even if it costs me my life, I must see The Swami."

Everyone was impressed with Mrs. Rothstein's determination and grit. How could such a woman, middle-aged and scrawny, find it in herself to brave man and beast, the jungle's sweltering heat and the mountain's numbing cold, in order to reach the swami?

With word of mouth as her only map, she slowly made her way up the Himalayan foothills until she found the great man's cavern. Outside sat his disciples, dressed in the traditional saffron robe of the Buddhist monk, their heads shaved bald.

They stared at Mrs. Rothstein.

"What is it you want, oh Woman from the Great Beyond?"

She said, "Listen, I've got to see The Swami. I won't leave until I do."

Knowing she was dead serious, they welcomed her in.

Enter she did, and stared intensely at the swami in his robes and turban, bathed in clouds of incense. And she said, "All right, Melvin. Enough with this swami silliness. Come on home."

GURU, INC.

VP PARABLES

VP ALLEGORIES

VP ENIGMAS

VP RIDDLES

corbett

Jack Corbett

"O Deep Thought computer," he said, "the task we have designed you to perform is this. We want you to tell us...." he paused, "The Answer."

"The Answer?" said Deep Thought. "The Answer to what?"

"Life!" urged Fook.

"The Universe!" said Lunkwill.

"Everything!" they said in chorus.

Deep Thought paused for a moment's reflection.

"Tricky," he said finally.

"But can you do it?"

Again, a significant pause. "Yes," said Deep Thought, "I can do it."

"There is an answer?" said Fook with breathless excitement.

"Yes," said Deep Thought. "Life, the Universe, and Everything. There is an answer. But, I'll have to think about it."

"How long?" he said.

"Seven and a half million years," said Deep Thought.

[SEVEN AND A HALF MILLION YEARS LATER.]

"Er... good morning, O Deep Thought" said Loonquawl nervously, "do you have...er, that is..."

"An Answer for you?" interrupted Deep Thought majestically. "Yes, I have."

The two men shivered with expectancy. Their waiting had not been in vain.

"There really is one?" breathed Phouchg.

"There really is one," confirmed Deep Thought.

"To Everything? To the great Question of Life, the Universe and Everything?"

"Yes.... though I don't think," added Deep Thought, "that you're going to like it."

"Doesn't matter!" said Phouchg. "We

"I always answer their questions with a question —it drives them nuts!"

Jack Corbett

must know it! Now!...."

"Now?" inquired Deep Thought.

"Yes! Now..."

"All right," said the computer, and settled into silence again. The two men fidgeted. The tension was unbearable.

"You're really not going to like it," observed Deep Thought.

"Tell us!"

"All right," said Deep Thought. "The Answer to the Great Question..."

"Yes..!"

"Of Life, the Universe and Everything..." said Deep Thought.

"Yes...!"

"Is..." said Deep Thought, and paused.

"Yes...!"

"Is..."

"Yes...!!!...?"

"Forty-two," said Deep Thought, with infinite majesty and calm.

"Forty-two!" yelled Loonquawl. "Is that all you've got to show for seven and a half million years' work?"

"I checked it very thoroughly," said the computer, "and that quite definitely is the answer. I think the problem, to be quite honest with you, is that you've never actually known what the question is."

—Douglas Adams, *The Hitcthhiker's Guide to the Galaxy*

18

"You can tell us the sound of one hand clapping
here, or you can tell us downtown."

Paul Noth

off the mark.com   by Mark Parisi

I CAN'T DECIDE ON A RINGTONE...
IT'S BETWEEN A TREE FALLING IN
THE FOREST AND ONE HAND CLAPPING...

Mark Parisi

OOOMMM   MMMOOOO

Mischa Richter

GOD'S CHILDREN

They're like cats... if they're in they want out, if they're out they want in...

YOU'D THINK THEY'D BE HAPPY IN HEAVEN, BUT THEY'RE LIKE KIDS-- NOTHING TO DO AND THEY GET BORED AND WHINY. SO I CAME UP WITH REINCARNATION JUST TO GET THEM OUT OF MY HAIR.

Hilary Price

Two octogenarians sit on a park bench. One asks the other: "Do you believe in an afterlife?"

"Well, Bert," replies Harry, "who's to say?"

"Maybe we ought to start thinking about it," says Bert. "Just in case, let's agree that whoever goes first, if he makes it to the other side — if there is another side— will find a way of getting a message to whoever's left behind."

Harry agrees.

One month later, Bert dies peacefully in his sleep. A few weeks later, Harry is sitting alone on the very same park bench. He hears a voice, as though from afar.

"Harry, Harry, can you hear me?" the voice says. "It's Bert."

"Bert, for heaven's sake, you made it, you crossed over! What's it like?"

"You wouldn't believe it, Harry. It's beautiful. There are azure skies, a soft breeze, sunshine all the time."

"Sounds nice," says Harry, "but what do you do all day?"

"Well," explains Bert, "we get up with the sun, eat some good breakfast, and there's nothing but making love until noon. After a delicious lunch, we nap until two and then make love again until about five. After a nutritious dinner, we go at it again until we fall asleep around 11."

"Wow!" says Harry, "Heaven sounds great!!"

"Who said anything about Heaven? I'm a rabbit in southern California."

One Hindu says to another, "Hey, how's life?"

The second Hindu replies, "I've had better."

Boy to his grandfather: "Yeah, well I didn't believe in reincarnation when I was your age either."

Hey, did you hear reincarnation's making a comeback?

What did the Dalai Lama say to the hot dog vendor?

"Make me one with everything."

Then the vendor prepared the hot dog and handed it to the Dalai Lama, who paid with a $20 bill. The vendor put the bill in his cash box and closed it. "Excuse me, but where's my change?" asked the Dalai Lama.

The vendor replied, "Change must come from within."

A gun then extended from the Dalai Lama's chest and he asked again, "Where's my change!?!"

The vendor said, "Whoa, man, where did that come from?"

The Dalai Lama replied, "This is my inner piece."

"It appears to be Siva, manifesting himself as Lord of Destruction, but why he's in Hartsdale on a Thursday night is beyond me."

Lee Lorenz

An aspiring monk asked to enter a monastery and attach himself to a guru. "Very well," said the guru, "but all students here observe the vow of silence. You will be allowed to speak only once every twelve years." The disciple agreed and took his vows.

After the first twelve years, the disciple said, "The bed's too hard."

After another twelve years, he said, "The food is lousy."

Twelve more years later, after thirty-six years of hard work and meditation, he said, "I quit."

"Good!" snapped his guru. "All you ever do is complain."

Another Zen student asked his master, "Is it okay to use e-mail?"

"Yes," replied the master, "but no attachments."

My karma just ran over your dogma.

Did you hear about the Buddhist who refused novocaine during a root canal?
—His goal: transcend dental medication.

A Zen student goes to a temple and asks how long it will take him to gain enlightenment if he becomes a disciple.

"Ten years," says the Zen master.

"Well, how about if I really work hard and double my effort?"

To which the master replies: "Twenty years."

I don't know about you, but I'd feel safer with an invisible magic person in the sky than I do with this volcano.

Dan Piraro

"G od is a great humorist. He just has a slow audience to work with."
—Garrison Keillor

"S uppose the world was only one of God's jokes. Would you work any the less to make it a good joke, instead of a bad one?"
—George Bernard Shaw

M oses to God: "Wait a minute, let me get this straight. They get to keep the oil and we cut off the tip of our WHAT?"

G od @TheTweetOfGod: The last people legitimately on a mission from Me were named Jake and Elwood.
—David Javerbaum, *An Act of God*

I f you want to make God laugh, tell Him your plans. —Yiddish proverb.

"I f there were no God, it would be necessary to invent him."
—Voltaire

"I t is the final proof of God's omnipotence that he need not exist in order to save us."
—Peter De Vries

"B eckett does not believe in God, though he seems to imply that God has committed an unforgivable sin by not existing."
—Anthony Burgess

"If by *Godot* I had meant *God* I would have said *God*, and not *Godot*."
—Samuel Beckett

O ne goldfish to its tank mate: "If there's no God, where do all these flakes come from?"

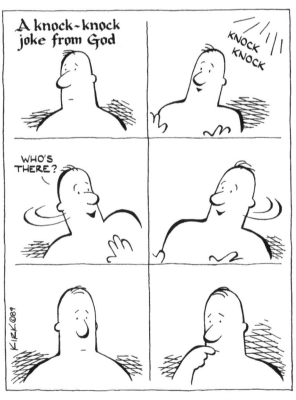

A knock-knock joke from God

KNOCK KNOCK

WHO'S THERE?

Kirk Anderson

"If you laugh at all of God's jokes,
he's never going to learn what's funny."

Kanin

Zach Kanin

"When you come right down to it, there are only four basic prayers: Gimme! Thanks! Oops! and Wow!"
— Rabbi Marc Gellman

A poor man was trying to understand the nature of God and so he asked Him, "God, is it true that to you a thousand years is but a minute?"

"Yes, my son."

"And God," continued the poor man, "is it true that to you a million dollars is but a penny?"

"Yes, my son."

"God..."

"Yes, my son?"

"May I have a penny?"

Pause.

"In a minute."

If you're chatting with God and He sneezes, what do you say?

Dan Piraro

WHY GOD DIDN'T GET TENURE

- He had only one major publication.
- It wasn't even written in English.
- It had no references and all His results came without proofs.
- It wasn't published in a refereed journal.
- Some even doubt He wrote it Himself.
- The scientific community has had a hard time replicating His results.
- He never applied to the Ethics Board for permission to use human subjects.
- When one experiment went awry, He tried to cover it up by drowning the subjects.
- He would not tolerate criticism and had no record of collegiality.
- He rarely came to class and instead just told the students to read the book.
- There are reports that He once sent his son to teach His class for Him.
- He expelled His first two students for knowing too much.
- He used obsolete teaching methods, such as peer pressure and guilt manipulation.
- He insisted on using only pass/fail grades instead of the standard A to F system.
- Although there were only ten requirements, most students failed His tests.
- His office hours were infrequent and usually held on a mountaintop.
- Even if He did create the world, what's He done lately?

In the beginning there was nothing. God said, "Let there be light!" And there was light. There was still nothing, but you sure could see it a whole lot better.

INFIDEL, n. In New York, one who does not believe in the Christian religion; in Constantinople, one who does.
—Ambrose Bierce, *The Devil's Dictionary* (1911)

God used to be an atheist, but then He read a self-help book and really started to believe in Himself.

Did you hear about the dyslexic atheist?
—He didn't believe in dog.

"Not only is there no God, but try getting a plumber on weekends."
—Woody Allen

Atheism is a non-prophet organization.

God @TheTweetOfGod
Yes, I'm pro-life. But if you're familiar with my work you know I'm not exactly anti-death either.
—David Javerbaum, *An Act of God*

"I love your early work."

Emily Flake

"When you get a chance, remember to ask God the meaning of life—it's a riot."

Zach Kanin

Little Johnny, aged five, was bending over a sheet of paper, intently focused, guiding his pencil ever so carefully. His mother, smiling at him fondly, said "What are you drawing?"

"A picture of God," said Johnny, without looking up.

"But, Johnny, nobody knows what God looks like," said his mother.

And Johnny said, "They will once I'm finished."

Did you hear the latest about God?
—She's black.

Robin Williams:
Tom Waits once said, "Maybe there's no devil; it's just God when He's drunk."

If God drinks, do you think God also gets stoned once in a while? Look at the platypus. I think so. God's up there going [*toking on a joint*] "Okay, let's take a beaver. Okay, let's put on a duck's bill… Hey, I'm God, what are you gonna do about it?"

Steven Wright:
If God dropped acid, would he see people?

*"I can't deal with any famines, massacres, or epidemics right now
—I've got to help some guy sink a foul shot."*

Robert Mankoff

A terrible storm was coming, and the government sent out flood warnings ordering the town to evacuate. The town preacher decided to stay, telling himself, "I believe in God. God will save me." The streets began to fill with water.

The preacher's neighbors drove past in a truck, shouting, "We have room for you; come with us and escape the flooding!" To which the preacher replied, "Thank you, but I'll stay here. I know that God will save me."

The waters soon rose higher, and the preacher had to retreat to the second floor of his home.

Looking out the window, he saw another neighbor, rowing by in a small boat. The neighbor said, "Come with me! I can get you to safety." The preacher refused, saying, "God will save me."

The floodwaters continued to rise, and the preacher had to climb up onto his roof.

A helicopter hovered overhead, and dropped down a rope ladder. "You have to climb up. We can save you, but it's now or never." The preacher again refused, insisting that God would save him.

Finally, the waters rose and swept the preacher away and drowned him. When he reached heaven, he asked God, "I trusted in You. Why didn't You save me?"

God replied, "I sent a truck, a boat, and a helicopter. What more did you want?!"

"Malt does more than Milton can
To justify God's ways to Man."
—A.E. Housman

The cares of the universe had been resting more heavily than usual on God's shoulders, and He frankly confessed the need for a rest.

"Why don't you take a short vacation, Boss" suggested the archangel Gabriel.

"Yes, but where?"

"How about that little place, Earth? You haven't been there in ages."

God shuddered. "No, no. It's a world of busybodies. I was there two thousand years ago and that's enough, thank you. I had an affair with a little Jewish girl and they're still talking about it down there."

Did you hear about the elderly Jewish gentleman who, on his deathbed, sent for a priest, declaring to his astonished relatives that he wanted to convert?

Asked why he would become a Catholic, after living all his life as a Jew, he answered: "Better one of them should die than one of us."

"I don't want to achieve immortality through my work. I want to achieve immortality through not dying."
—Woody Allen

"We have no reliable guarantee that the afterlife will be any less exasperating than this one, have we?"
—Noel Coward

It is better never to have been born, but who among us has such luck?

Voltaire on his death bed, asked by a priest to denounce Satan:
"Now, now, my good man, this is no time to make new enemies."

Oscar Wilde, nearing the end in a tawdry Paris hotel room:
"This wallpaper and I are fighting a duel to the death. Either it goes or I do."

What no one ever said on their death bed: "I should have bought more crap."

Heck is reserved for those who don't believe in Gosh.

I'm planning on living forever, and so far it's working.

"I'm going to live forever, or die trying."
—Joseph Heller, *Catch-22*

I don't want to live forever, but I also don't want to die forever.

"I do not believe in an afterlife, although I am bringing a change of underwear."
—Woody Allen

Jack Ziegler

"Well, it __was__ original."

Mick Stevens

"Adam & Eve had many advantages, but the principal one was that they escaped teething."
—Mark Twain

Jesus was having a final dinner with his disciples on that fateful night, exactly in the tableau immortalized by Leonardo da Vinci. As they gathered reverentially around him, he looked about at them.

There was Judas Iscariot who, Jesus knew, would betray him to the authorities before three hours had passed. And then there was Thomas who, on a crucial occasion, would express doubts. And of course there was Peter, the prince of the disciples who, as he well knew, would deny him thrice ere the cock crowed.

There seemed only one thing to do. Jesus called over the head waiter. "Max," he said. "Separate checks."

"Christ died for our sins. Dare we make his martyrdom meaningless by not committing them?"
—Jules Feiffer, *Little Murders*

Jesus' greatest miracle was finding guys named Peter, John, James, Matthew, Andrew, Philip, and Thomas in the Middle East.

WHO WAS JESUS?

This question has plagued historians for centuries.

JESUS MUST HAVE BEEN BLACK BECAUSE:
• He called everyone "brother."
• He liked Gospel.
• He couldn't get a fair trial.

JESUS MUST HAVE BEEN JEWISH BECAUSE:
• He went into his father's business.
• He lived at home until he was 33.
• He was sure his mother was a virgin and his mother was sure he was God.

JESUS MUST HAVE BEEN ITALIAN BECAUSE:
• He talked with his hands.
• He had wine with every meal.
• He worked in construction.

JESUS MUST HAVE BEEN PUERTO RICAN BECAUSE:
• His first name was Jesus.
• He was bilingual.
• He was always being harassed by the authorities.

JESUS MUST HAVE BEEN FROM CALIFORNIA BECAUSE:
• He never cut his hair.
• He walked around barefoot all the time.
• He started a new religion.

JESUS MUST HAVE BEEN IRISH BECAUSE:
• He never got married.
• He was always telling stories.
• He loved green pastures

BUT THE MOST COMPELLING EVIDENCE OF ALL —3 PROOFS THAT JESUS WAS A WOMAN:
• She had to feed a crowd at a moment's notice when there was no food.
• She kept trying to get a message across to a bunch of men who just didn't get it.
• Even when she was dead, she had to get up because there was more work for her to do.

Which Religion is Right for You?

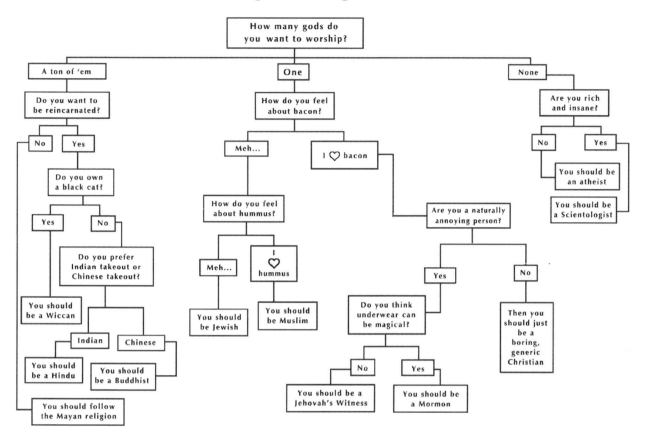

Mr. Jones had ordered a suit from a neighborhood tailor who had been highly recommended to him, but considerable time had passed and the suit had not yet been delivered. Visibly upset, Jones stepped into the tailor's shop to have it out. He said, "See here, Mr. Levy, you promised to let me have the suit in two weeks, and four weeks have already passed."

"I'm working. I'm working," said Mr. Levy. "The suit is hanging right there. It's almost finished."

"Almost finished? But why does it take you so long, Mr. Levy? The good Lord made the whole world in only six days."

Mr. Levy put down his needle, stood up tall, and said, "Come here, mister. I want you should feel the material on this suit I am making for you. Notice the fine cut, the silk lining, the master stitching. Double stitching on the seams, mind you. Okay? Now I want you should come to the window."

"So?"

"So?? So look at this suit ... and look at the world!"

"I sometimes think that God in creating man somewhat overestimated his ability."
  —Oscar Wilde

What do you get when you cross a Lutheran and a Buddhist?
—Someone who sits up all night worrying about nothing.

SHIT HAPPENS IN VARIOUS WORLD RELIGIONS

TAOISM: Shit happens.

CONFUCIANISM: Confucius say "Shit happens."

BUDDHISM: Shit happens, but it isn't really shit.

HINDUISM: This shit happened before.

HARE KRISHNA: Shit happens, rama rama, hare hare.

ISLAM: If shit happens, it is the will of Allah.

QUAKERS: Let us not fight over this shit.

PROTESTANTISM: Shit won't happen if you work harder.

ATHEISM: I can't believe this shit!

CATHOLICISM: If shit happens, you deserved it.

JUDAISM: Why does shit always happen to us?

TELEVANGELISM: Your tax-deductible donation will make this shit stop happening.

JEHOVAH'S WITNESSES: Knock-knock, shit happens.

RASTAFARIANISM: Let's smoke this shit!

Mark Parisi

John Callahan

A priest, a rabbi and an imam walk into a bar. The bartender asks, "What is this, some kind of joke?"

In these troubling times it is important for all of us, of all faiths, to recognize these four Religious Verities:

Muslims do not recognize Jews as God's chosen people.

Jews do not recognize Jesus as the Messiah.

Protestants do not recognize the Pope as the leader of the Christian world.

Baptists do not recognize each other at Hooters.

"The difference between a Northern Baptist and a Southern Baptist is a Northern Baptist says, 'There ain't no hell.' And a Southern Baptist says, 'The hell there ain't!'"
—Brother Dave Gardner

How do you get a Unitarian family to move out of the neighborhood?
—Burn a question mark on their lawn.

Wearing a t-shirt with "Let's talk about God" on it will pretty much guarantee you a seat to yourself on the train.

"I can guess that you're a holy man," Tom divined.

- "Adam, there appears to be an apple missing," God insinuated.
- "There is no true happiness without a belief in God," Tom preached diagnostically.
- "Argh! Father, forgive them, for they know not what they do," said Jesus crossly.
- "Adherents of my religion don't all have to believe the same thing," Tom decreed.

How many ancient philosophers does it take to screw in a lightbulb?
—Four. One to screw in the lightbulb and three to say "Yes, Socrates," "Well done, Socrates," "Good job, Socrates."

- How many medieval philosophers does it take to screw in a lightbulb?
  —Two. One to screw in the lightbulb and one to check what Aristotle said about screwing in lightbulbs.
- How many nihilists does it take to screw in a lightbulb?
  —Vats ze point?? It vill just go kaput again!!
- How many analytic philosophers does it take to screw in a lightbulb?
  —None. It is a pseudo-problem. Lightbulbs give off light, hence the name. If the bulb were broken and wasn't giving off light, it wouldn't be a lightbulb, now would it?
- How many logical positivists does it take to screw in a lightbulb?
  —A priori, we can't tell.
- How many fallibilists does it take to screw in a lightbulb?
  —Three, but I could be wrong about that.
- How many Zen masters does it take to change a lightbulb?
  —None. Change must come from within.
  —Three. One to change the lightbulb, one not to change the lightbulb, and one to neither change nor not change the lightbulb.

- How many existentialists does it take to screw in a lightbulb?
  — Two. One to screw it in and one to observe how the lightbulb itself symbolizes a single incandescent beacon of subjective reality in a netherworld of endless absurdity reaching out toward a maudlin cosmos of nothingness.
- How many New Agers does it take to screw in a lightbulb?
  —None. They just start a "Coping with Darkness" support group.
- How many atheists does it take to screw in a lightbulb?
  —Irrelevant. They shall forever remain in darkness.
- How many philosophy professors does it take to screw in a lightbulb?
  —Three: one to screw in the lightbulb and two to debate whether they ought to, and if so, whether it follows that they can.

Andy Singer

31

Chapter Two

Merely a Ph.D.

The Ups and Downs of Higher Education

"Daddy works in a magical, faraway land called Academia."

David Sipress

"Certainly. A party of four at seven-thirty in the name of Dr. Jennings. May I ask whether that is an actual medical degree or merely a Ph.D.?"

JB Handelsman

After the outbreak of the First World War in 1914, a young woman accosted a Cambridge don in the street. "And what are you doing to defend civilization?" she demanded.

"Madam," he replied, "I am the civilization that is being defended."

Birmingham, England; 1953.
A Pakistani enters a hotel to book a room. "Just put your cross here," says the receptionist.

The Pakistani puts two crosses.

"What's the second cross for?" asks the receptionist.

"Oh, that's my Ph.D. from Oxford."

Four college classmates go out of town to party for the weekend instead of studying for a big exam on Monday. A bit wasted and hoping for a make-up test they could actually prepare for, they scheme to return on Tuesday, armed with dated receipts for motel and gas expenses. They explain that the car got a flat tire and that they didn't have a spare.

The professor agrees to give them a make-up exam the next day, so that night they actually study. When the time comes, the students take their seats in separate corners of the exam room, and the professor explains that the exam will be in the form of a single question.

They settle in, still silently enjoying their own cleverness —until the professor writes on the blackboard: "Which tire?"

Merely a Ph.D.

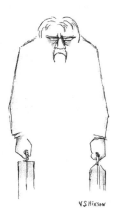

Professor Zack returns from a sabbatical in England, France, and Italy, equipped with a refreshingly new perspective on his position at Midsouthern University.

Vivian Hixson

FIRST PROFESSOR: Say, Rodney, have you read Taylor's *The Malaise of Modernity*?

SECOND PROFESSOR: Read it? I haven't even taught it.

In anticipation of one of the periodic Stalinist purges, a certain Mr. Cohen of Kiev thought it prudent to study dialectical materialism. Not able to make heads or tails out of it, he confers with his rabbi.

"Dialectics?" says the rabbi. "Easy. I'll explain it to you. Two chimney sweeps fall down a chimney into the fireplace. One is clean, the other is black with soot. Which one goes to wash himself?"

"The dirty one, of course."

"Wrong! The dirty one sees the clean one and thinks he is clean too. The clean one sees the other covered with soot, so he goes to wash. Now let's try it again. Two chimney sweeps fall down a chimney. One is clean, the other is dirty. Which one goes to wash?"

"Why, you just said the clean one!"

"Wrong! Each one looks at his hands, and the one with the dirty hands goes to wash himself. Try again. Two chimney sweeps fall down a chimney. Which one goes to wash himself?"

"All right, the dirty one then!"

"Wrong! Neither. The dirty one sees the clean one, and the clean one looks at his own hands. Try again. Two chimney sweeps..."

"Stop, Rabbi, stop!!" cries Cohen. "You're simply twisting things to make it come out whichever way you want."

"Now you've got the idea!" says the rabbi. "That's what dialectics is all about."

Calvin and Hobbes

CALVIN AND HOBBES © 1993 Watterson. Reprinted with permission of UNIVERSAL UCLICK. All rights reserved.

Bill Watterson

DREAMS OF ACADEMIC GLORY

Thrilled by the last lecture, the class rises in spontaneous applause.

Vivian Hixson

The professor who comes to class ten minutes late is rare. In fact, he's in a class by himself.

"A professor is someone who talks in someone else's sleep."
— W.H. Auden

And then there was the absent-minded professor who forgot to write a $75 textbook and sell it to his class.

VISITING LECTURER, AFTER A LONG-WINDED SPEECH: I may have run a bit over, but I haven't a watch.
STUDENT, FROM REAR OF ROOM. There's a calendar on the wall behind you.

An engineer was summoned to a local college dormitory on a cold winter night because one of its boilers had ceased to function and the maintenance staff could not pinpoint the problem. When the engineer arrived, the anxious Dean of Students took him right to the basement. The engineer leaned into the boiler, examined the situation, made one tap with his hammer, pulled his head out, and said, "She should work now." And indeed it did.

Later that week, the college received a bill for $1,050.50. Outraged, the dean called the engineer to protest. "How can you submit such a ridiculous bill?"

"Well," explained the engineer, "the fifty bucks is my regular service fee: that's for showing up. Fifty cents is for that one hammer tap. And the thousand dollars is for knowing where to tap."

Merely a Ph.D.

ACADEMIC PHRASES: A TRANSLATION

"It has long been known…"
  —I didn't look up the original reference.

"A definite trend is evident …"
  —This data is practically meaningless.

"While it has not been possible to provide definite answers to the questions …"
  —An unsuccessful experiment, but I still hope to get it published.

"Three of the samples were chosen for detailed study …"
  —The other results didn't make any sense.

"These results will be discussed in a subsequent report …"
  —I might get around to this sometime, if funded.

"In my experience …"
  —Once.

"In case after case …"
  —Twice.

"In a series of cases …"
  —Thrice.

"It is believed that …"
  —I think.

"It is generally believed that …"
  —A couple of others think so too.

"Correct within an order of magnitude …"
  —Wrong.

"A statistically-oriented projection of the significance of these findings …"
  —A wild guess.

"A careful analysis of obtainable data …"
  —Three pages of notes were obliterated when I knocked over a glass of iced tea.

"It is clear that much additional work will be required before a complete understanding of this phenomenon can be reached …"
  —I don't understand it.

"After additional study by my colleagues …"
  —They don't understand it either.

"Thanks are due to Rob Demarest for assistance with the experiment and to Sophie Adams for valuable discussions …"
  —Demarest did the work and Adams explained to me what it meant.

"A highly significant area for exploratory study."
  —A totally useless topic chosen by my committee.

"It is hoped that this study will stimulate further investigation in this field …"
  —I quit.

"My office door is always open; however, I'm rarely there."

Andrew Toos

Merely a Ph.D.

"He taught us a game he claims to have invented, called *Humiliation* … a game you won by humiliating yourself… Each person names a book which he hasn't read but assumes the others have read, and scores a point for every person who has read it. Get it? Well, Howard Ringbaum didn't. You know Howard, he has a pathological urge to succeed and a pathological fear of being thought uncultured, and this game sets his two obsessions at war with each other, because he could succeed in the game only by exposing a gap in his culture. At first his psyche just couldn't absorb the paradox and he named some 18th-century book so obscure I can't even remember the name of it. Of course, he came last in the final score, and sulked. It was a stupid game, he said, and refused to play the next round … but I could see he was following the play attentively, knitting his brows and twisting his napkin in his fingers as the point of the game began to dawn on him. It's quite a groovy game, actually, a kind of intellectual strip poker. For instance, it came out that Luke Hogan had never read *Paradise Regained*. I mean, I know it isn't his field, but to think you can get to be Chairman of the English Department at Euphoric State without ever having read *Paradise Regained* makes you think, right? I could see Howard taking this in, going a bit pale when he realized that Luke was telling the truth. Well, on the third round, Sy was leading the field with *Hiawatha*, Mr. Swallow being the only other person who hadn't read it, when suddenly Howard slammed his fist on the table, jutted his jaw about six feet over the table, and said:

'Hamlet!'

Well, of course, we all laughed, not very much because it didn't seem much of a joke. In fact it wasn't a joke at all. Howard admitted to having seen the Laurence Olivier movie, but insisted he had never read the text of *Hamlet*. Nobody believed him of course, and this made him as sore as hell. He said did we think he was lying, and Sy more or less implied that we did … Howard Ringbaum unexpectedly flunked his review three days later and it's generally supposed that this

Dan Piraro

was because the English Department dared not give tenure to a man who had publicly admitted to not having read *Hamlet*."

—David Lodge, *Changing Places*

NIGHTMARE FINAL-EXAM QUESTIONS

- BIOLOGY: Create life. Estimate the differences in subsequent human culture if this life form had developed 500,000 years earlier, with special attention to the probable effect, if any, on the English parliamentary system circa 1750. Prove your thesis.

- PRE-MED: You will be provided with a rusty razor blade, a piece of gauze, and a full bottle of Scotch. Remove your appendix. Don't suture until your work has been inspected. You have 15 minutes.

- ELECTRICAL ENGINEERING: You will be placed in a nuclear reactor and given a partial copy of the electrical layout. The electrical

DOONESBURY © 1985 G. B. Trudeau. Reprinted with permission of UNIVERSAL UCLICK. All rights reserved.

G.B. Trudeau

system has been tampered with. You have seventeen minutes to find the problem and correct it before the reactor melts down. (*Not* a simulation.)

- HISTORY: Describe the history of the papacy from its origins to the present day, concentrating on its social, political, economic, religious, and philosophical impact on Europe, America, Asia, and Africa. Be brief and concise, yet specific.

- PUBLIC SPEAKING: The Four Horsemen of the Apocalypse are storming the classroom. Calm them. You may use any ancient language except Latin, Hebrew, or Greek.

- COMPUTER SCIENCE: Write a fifth-generation computer language. Using this language, write a computer program to finish the rest of this exam for you.

- MUSIC: Write a full piano concerto. Orchestrate and perform it with a clarinet and drum. You will find a piano under your seat. You will need to tune it.

- PSYCHOLOGY: Based on your knowledge of their early works, evaluate the emotional stability, degree of adjustment, and repressed frustrations of each of the following: Alexander of Aphrodisias, Ramses II, and Gregory of Nicea. Support your evaluation with quotations from each man's work. It is not necessary to translate.

- CHEMISTRY: You must identify a poison antidote, which you will find at your lab table. There are two beakers, only one of which holds the antidote. If the wrong substance is used, it causes instant death. You may begin as soon as the professor injects you with a sample of the poison.

Merely a Ph.D.

THE EVOLUTION OF THE PROFESSOR

Adjunct   Assistant   Associate   Tenured Professor

Francis Acupan

"An intellectual is a man who takes more words than necessary to tell more than he knows."
—Dwight D. Eisenhower

"It must be admitted that even among intellectuals there are some really intelligent people."
—Mikhail Bulgakov

"Intellectuals are like the Mafia; they only kill their own."
—Woody Allen

"We should take care not to make the intellect our god; it has, of course, powerful muscles, but no personality."
—Albert Einstein

"I know as well as anyone that the intellectual is a dangerous animal, ever ready to betray."
—Albert Camus

"There's always something suspect about an intellectual on the winning side."
—Vaclav Havel

"The intellect is a very nice whirligig toy, but how people take it seriously is more than I can understand."
—Ezra Pound

"The intellect is not a serious thing, and never has been. It is an instrument on which one plays, that is all."
—Oscar Wilde

"SINCE GREG WAS ACCEPTED BY MENSA, HE'D RATHER NOT SAY ANYTHING THAN SAY SOMETHING INCORRECT."

Sidney Harris

Merely a Ph.D.

Alternative I.Q. Test

1. How do you put a giraffe into a refrigerator?
Answer: Open the refrigerator, put in the giraffe, and close the door. This question tests whether you tend to do simple things in an overly complicated way.

2. How do you put an elephant into a refrigerator?
Did you say: open the refrigerator, put in the elephant, and close the refrigerator? Wrong answer.
Answer: Open the refrigerator, take out the giraffe, put in the elephant and close the door. This tests your ability to think through the repercussions of your previous actions.

3. The Lion King is hosting an animal conference. All the animals attend… except one. Which animal does not attend?
Answer: The Elephant. The elephant is in the refrigerator. You just put him in there. This tests your memory.

Okay, even if you did not answer the first three questions correctly, you still have one more chance to show your true abilities.

4. There is a river you must cross but it is used by crocodiles, and you do not have a boat. How do you manage it?
Answer: You jump into the river and swim across. Have you not been listening? All the crocodiles are attending the animal conference. This tests whether you learn quickly from your mistakes.

"Personally, I'm waiting for caller IQ."
—Sandra Bernhard

"Education consists mainly of what we have unlearned."
—Mark Twain

"The fellow who thinks he knows it all is especially annoying to those of us who do."
—Harold Coffin

S. Harris

"You can't build a hut, you don't know how to find edible roots and you know nothing about predicting the weather. In other words, you do terribly on our I.Q. test."

Sidney Harris

"It ain't what a man don't know that makes him a fool, but what he does know that ain't so."
—Josh Billings

"Half of being smart is knowing what you are dumb about."
—Solomon Short

Charting the Intellectual Growth Rings of Fred P. Dobbler, Baby Boomer
DATES & MAJOR INFLUENCES:
1959: Howdy Doody
1961: Captain Kangaroo
1963: The Three Stooges
1965: Fred Flintstone
1967-69: Star Trek
1971: Twilight Zone reruns
1972: Watergate Hearings (forced to watch by politically active girlfriend).
1979: J.R. Ewing, Mork, Ayatollah Khomeini
1975-78: Star Trek reruns
1980-90: MTV, Wheel of Fortune, Ronald Reagan

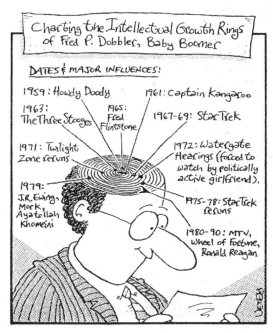

Bradford Veley

 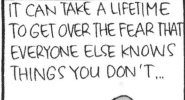 

Hilary Price

The Lone Ranger and Tonto were camping in the wilderness. After they got their tent set up, both men fell sound asleep. Some hours later, Tonto wakes the Lone Ranger and says, "Kemo Sabe, look towards sky, what you see?"

The Lone Ranger replies, "I see millions of stars."

"What that tell you?" asked Tonto.

The Lone Ranger ponders for a minute and then says, "Astronomically-speaking, it tells me there are millions of galaxies and potentially billions of planets. Astrologically, it tells me that Saturn is in Leo. Time-wise, it appears to be approximately a quarter past three in the morning. Theologically, the Lord is all-powerful and we are small and insignificant. Meteorologically, it seems we will have a beautiful day tomorrow. What does it tell you, Tonto?"

"You dumber than buffalo," says Tonto. "It mean someone stole tent."

"The more you read, the more you know. The more you know, the smarter you grow." —Dr. Seuss

"Why study? The more we learn, the more we forget. The more we forget, the less we know. The less we know, the less we forget. The less we forget, the more we know. Why study?" —Milton Berle

BRAINS

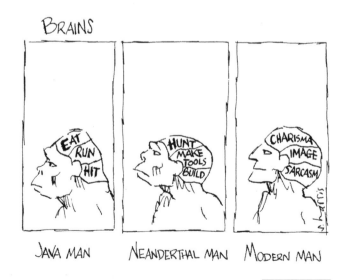

JAVA MAN   NEANDERTHAL MAN   MODERN MAN

Sidney Harris

A guy is driving through the back woods of Montana when he sees a sign in front of a broken-down shanty: 'TALKING DOG FOR SALE." Skeptical but curious, he rings the bell. The owner appears and tells him the dog is in the backyard, so the guy goes back there and sees a nice-looking Labrador Retriever.

"You talk?" he asks incredulously.

"Yep," the Labrador replies.

After the guy recovers from the shock of hearing a dog talk, he says "So, what's your story?"

The Lab looks up and says, "Well, I discovered that I could talk when I was pretty young. I wanted to serve our country, so I told the CIA. Soon I was jetting all around the globe, sitting in rooms with spies and world leaders. No one figured a dog would be eavesdropping.

"I was one of their most valuable spies for eight years running. But the jetting around really tired me out, and I knew I wasn't getting any younger, so I decided to settle down, and took a job at the airport doing undercover security. I'd wander over to some suspicious characters, wag my tail, and listen in. I uncovered some evil doings and was awarded a batch of medals. But eventually I got hitched, had a mess of puppies, and now I'm just retired."

The guy is amazed. He goes back in and asks the owner what he wants for the dog.

"Ten dollars," the owner says.

"Ten dollars? This dog is amazing! Why on earth are you selling him so cheap?"

"Because he's a liar. He never did any of that shit."

"There is nothing so stupid as an educated man, if you get him off the thing he was educated in."
　　—Will Rogers`

"Intellectual brilliance is no guarantee against being dead wrong."
　　—David Fasold

ON MY VCR I TAPE "NOVA" ON GENE-SPLICING.

I TAPE THE METROPOLITAN OPERA PRODUCTION OF "THE RING CYCLE."

I TAPE THE ROYAL SHAKESPEARE PRODUCTION OF "OEDIPUS THE KING."

WHILE I **WATCH** BASEBALL, BASKETBALL, "WHEEL OF FORTUNE" AND "JEOPARDY."

I NEVER WATCH THE SHOWS I TAPE.

BUT I FEEL LESS STUPID KNOWING MY VCR IS AN INTELLECTUAL.

Jules Feiffer

A professor driving through Arkansas got lost on a narrow, bumpy back-country road and was soon passing a pig farm. Suddenly, his eye caught something really strange. He did a double-take, muttered to himself, and then looked a third time. He wondered if he had seen correctly —it looked like a pig with a wooden leg!

Spotting the farmer nearby, he called out. "Excuse me, I was just driving by and I noticed something that I just had to stop and ask about. Tell me, did I see right? Is there really a pig over there with a wooden leg?"

The farmer smiled, a mischievous twinkle in his eye. "Yep, that would be old Caesar you were seeing. He's the finest pig a man could ever hope to have —and smart! Now, I can tell you're an educated fellow, and you probably never thought of pigs being particularly smart, but old Caesar there, well… you see that barge down on the river? That's a mining dredge, taking out platinum ore. Old Caesar sniffed out the vein and now that dredge brings me in nearly a hundred thousand bucks a year."

Warming to the tale, the farmer continued. "And over there in the meadow, you see those oil derricks? It was Caesar who showed them where to drill. Of course it's just a small operation, but I got a quarter of a million on the mineral lease."

The farmer had one more yarn in him. "There's another thing, a little more personal. One night a couple of years ago I got to drinking, and I guess I had more than I shoulda. I passed out drunk, fell down, knocked over a lamp. That started a fire in the house, and old Caesar smelled the smoke. He came in the back door, got the wife and kid out, roused me up, and got me out. There's no question about it —that night old Caesar saved all our lives, and you know, that is not the sort of thing a man is going to forget too easily."

"Why," the professor said, "this is all amazing! I have never heard of a pig like this before! This is fantastic! But tell me, how did he get that wooden leg? Was he in a wreck or something?"

The farmer laughed. "Well, naturally," he said, "when you have a pig that smart, you don't want to eat him all at once."

"WHAT EXACTLY DO YOU MEAN BY, 'NO CHEATING'?"

Mark Litzler

During an exam, a proctor spies a student cheating. Once the exam is over and the students are handing in their blue books, the proctor pulls the cheater aside: "I'll take that book, thank you very much. I saw you cheating."

The student stares the proctor right in the eye: "Cheating? Moi??" he says haughtily. "Do you have any idea who I am?"

"No," says the proctor.

"Perfect," says the student —and grabs the stack of blue books, throws them up in the air with his own, and runs from the room.

It was nearing exam time and the professor made it clear that it was time to start studying. "The examination is already in the hands of the printer," he said. "Are there any questions?"

A VOICE FROM THE REAR OF THE ROOM: "Yeah —what's the name of the printer?"

"I took one course in existential philosophy at New York University, and on the final they gave me ten questions, and I couldn't answer a single one of 'em... I left 'em all blank. I got a hundred."
—Woody Allen, *Stardust Memories*

off the mark.com
by Mark Parisi

MAY I RECOMMEND THE SEPTEMBER SPECIALS? WE HAVE HISTORY HOMEWORK WITH HOLLANDAISE AND A MATH HOMEWORK MARINADE... BOTH QUITE FRESH...

ATLANTIC FEATURE ©1994 MARK PARISI

offthemark.com

Mark Parisi

An attractive female student visits a young professor during his office hours. She glances down the hall, closes his door, kneels pleadingly. "I would do anything to pass this exam." She leans closer to him, flips back her hair, bats her eyelashes, and gazes soulfully into his eyes. "I mean..." she whispers, "...I would do... *anything*!!"

He returns her gaze. "Anything??"

"Yes... anything!!"

His voice turns to a whisper. "Would you... study???"

It was a week before Christmas and a college business student was taking his very last final exam. It consisted of a single question: "What factors cause an economic recession?"

Short on information but long on the spirit of the season, the student counted on a bit of professorial good will and wrote, "God only knows. I don't. Merry Christmas!"

When he got the paper back, there was a simple notation in the margin:

"God gets 100. You get 0. Happy New Year!!"

Calvin and Hobbes

WHAT DOES IT MEAN WHEN SOMEONE SAYS TO "GIVE IT THE OL' COLLEGE TRY"?

IT MEANS YOU JOIN YOUR FRIENDS, GET SOME CHEAP BEER, ORDER A PIZZA, AND FORGET ABOUT TOMORROW.

THAT'S NOT WHAT IT MEANS!

WHERE DID *YOU* GO TO COLLEGE?

NEVER MIND.

CALVIN AND HOBBES © 1995 Watterson. Reprinted with permission of UNIVERSAL UCLICK. All rights reserved.

Bill Watterson

45

Dan Piraro

LATE SHOW WITH DAVID LETTERMAN: TOP 10 COURSES FOR ATHLETES AT SMU

10. Subtraction: Addition's Tricky Pal

9. The first 30 Pages of *A Tale of Two Cities*: Foundation of a Classic

8. Sandwich-making (final project required)

7. Alumni-owned Hotels, Restaurants and Car Dealerships: The Interlocking Economy

6. Pre-Law Seminar: Age of Consent in the 50 States

5. The Denny's Menu: Recent Discoveries

4. The Bunny and the Wolf: Hand-Shadow Workshop

3. Draw Winky

2. From First Love to Looker: The Films in which Susan Dey Appears Naked

1. The Poetry of Hank Stram

A professor was giving a big exam to his students. He handed out all of the tests and went back to his desk to wait. Once the allotted time was over and the students had all handed the tests back in, the professor noticed that one of them had attached a $100 bill with a note saying, "A dollar per point."

The next class the professor handed the exams back. This student got back his test — and $64 change.

Said to be a true story:

A student was taking a class taught by Milton Friedman at the University of Chicago. After a late night diligently studying, he fell asleep in class. This sent Friedman into a tizzy and he came over and pounded on the student's desk, demanding an answer to a question he had just posed to the class. The student, shaken but suddenly wide awake, said "I'm sorry, Professor. I missed the question, but the answer is increase the money supply."

"You're the best teacher I've ever had. You opened my eyes to the world and showed me how to think critically... I was *happy* until I met *you*."

Loren Fishman

Dan Piraro

STUDENT EXCUSES FOR BEING ABSENT:

- Last night I set half the clocks in my house ahead an hour and the other half back an hour, and spent 18 hours in a space-time continuum loop, reliving yesterday-today (right up until the explosion). Accordingly, I will be in late, or early.

- I just found out that I was switched at birth. Legally, I shouldn't come to class knowing my student records may now contain false information.

- The dog ate my car keys. We're going to hitchhike to the vet.

- I am converting my calendar from Julian to Gregorian.

- I can't come to school today because the EPA has determined that my house is completely surrounded by wetlands and I have to arrange for helicopter transportation.

Apparently in a big rush, a college student who was shopping at a Cambridge, Massachusetts supermarket wheeled his overfilled cart into the "10 Items or Less" lane.

A no-nonsense woman, no doubt used to this kind of behavior, tapped him firmly on the shoulder. "What's the problem here, sonny boy?" she asked. "You go to Harvard and can't count or you go to M.I.T. and can't read?"

SCHOOL CHAPLAIN: I know there are those among you who drink. Let me be an example to you. There are twelve bars in town and I'm proud to say I've never been in one of them.

VOICE FROM THE REAR: Which one?

The frat boy's parents paid him a surprise late-night visit. In front of the Greek house, his father called out, "Is this where Robert Jones lives?"

VOICE FROM ON HIGH: Yeah —just throw him in.

Bradford Veley

"Thanks for waiting for me, Jocko, but I still can't play. I've decided to go for a Ph.D."

Leo Cullum

YOU JUST MIGHT BE A GRAD STUDENT IF:

- You are startled to meet people who have no desire to read.
- You have ever discussed academic matters at a sporting event.
- You actually have a preference between microfilm and microfiche.
- You regard Advil as a vitamin.
- You spend the only free time in your schedule complaining about how you have no free time in your schedule.
- You consider all papers to be works-in-progress.
- Professors don't really care when you turn in work anymore.
- You have given up trying to keep your books organized and are now just trying to keep them all in the same general area.
- You find the bibliographies of books more interesting than the actual text.

TOP TEN LIES TOLD BY GRAD STUDENTS

10. It doesn't bother me at all that my college roommate is making $110K a year on Wall Street.

9. I'd be delighted to proofread your book/chapter/article.

8. My work has a lot of practical importance.

7. I would never date an undergraduate.

6. Your latest article was so inspiring.

5. I turned down a lot of great job offers to come here.

4. I just have one more book to read and then I'll start writing.

3. The department is giving me so much support.

2. My job prospects look really good.

1. I'll be out of here in only two more years.

It's time to move out when Mom says,

Isabella Bannerman

Andy Singer

A Ph.D. student, a post-doc, and their professor are walking through a city park on their lunch break when they find an antique oil lamp. They rub it and a genie comes out in a puff of smoke.

The genie says, "I can only grant three wishes, so I'll give each of you just one."

"Me first! Me first!" says the Ph.D. student. "I want to be in the Bahamas, driving a speedboat with a gorgeous woman who sunbathes topless."

Poof! He's gone.

"Me next! Me next!" says the post-doc. "I want to be in Hawaii, relaxing on the beach with a professional hula dancer on one side and a Mai Tai on the other."

Poof! He's gone.

"You're next," the genie says to the professor.

The prof says, "I want those guys back in the lab after lunch."

Hilary Price

Merely a Ph.D.

David Sipress

Three academicians — one teaches engineering, one literature, and the third is the dean — are traveling in the countryside. Weary, they stop at a small country inn.

"I only have two tiny rooms, so one of you will have to sleep in the barn," the innkeeper says. The engineering professor volunteers to sleep in the barn, goes outside, and the others go to bed. In a short time they're awakened by a knock. It's the engineering professor, who says, "There's a cow in that barn. I'm a Hindu, and it would offend my beliefs to sleep next to a sacred animal."

The literature professor says that, OK, he'll sleep in the barn. The others go back to bed, but soon are awakened by another knock. It's the lit prof who says, "There's a pig in that barn. I'm Jewish, and cannot sleep next to an unclean animal."

So the dean is sent to the barn. It's getting late, the others are very tired and soon fall asleep. But they're awakened by an even louder knocking. They open the door and are surprised by what they see:

It's the cow and the pig.

Sᴀʏʀᴇ's Lᴀᴡ: In academia, the disputes are so bitter because the stakes are so small.

"A conference is a gathering of important people who singly can do nothing, but together can decide that nothing can be done."

—Fred Allen

"Hey, I've got it! The perfect formula! We put two full professors on the committee to give it clout, and a new assistant professor on so the work will get done."

Vivian Hixson

Merely a Ph.D.

"You might not know it now but I
used to have some great lesson plans."

Andrew Toos

The professor began his discussion of deductive logic with an example: "My father came to the United States during the Russian Revolution, my mother left Italy when Mussolini came to power, and I always wear an orange tie on Thursdays. From that information I assume we can all agree that it would be impossible to deduce exactly how old I am."

STUDENT: Sure, we can. You're 44.

PROFESSOR (*Astounded*): Right!! But how on earth did you figure that out?

STUDENT: I have a cousin who's 22 and he's only half as crazy.

PROFESSOR: Didn't you have a brother in this course last year?

STUDENT: No, sir, that was me. I'm taking the class over again.

PROFESSOR: Extraordinary resemblance, though. Extraordinary.

A professor runs into one of his students on the street. "Clarence," he demands, "why weren't you at my last biology class."

"But Professor Wilkins," says the student, "if I had known it was the last class I would definitely have been there."

A maiden at college named Breeze
  Weighed down by B.A.'s and Litt. D's
    Collapsed from the strain
    Alas, it was plain
  She was killing herself by degrees.

Andy Singer

Merely a Ph.D.

"Look, Harvey, the only reason you're depressed is that you're letting yourself be bound by conventional standards. I think that writing 5,383 multiple-choice questions is a contribution to literature."

Vivian Hixson

"The number of people not attending class today really bothers me," said the professor absent-mindedly.
- "Actually, I think the teacher didn't give enough exams," Tom protested.
- "This student appealed his grade, so I have to score his exam again," Tom remarked.
- "You are going to fail my class," said the teacher degradingly.
- "This is the first step towards my thesis," said Tom abstractly.
- "I can't help right now, I have to attend my Ph.D. oral examination," said Tom defensively.
- "Of course you graduated," said Tom diplomatically.
- "I teach at a university," Tom professed.
- "I have a B.A. in social work," said Tom with a degree of concern.

How many deans does it take to screw in a lightbulb?
—Two. One to assure the faculty that everything possible is being done to remedy the situation, and another to screw the bulb into a faucet.
- How many undergraduate students does it take to screw in a lightbulb?
—If it's not on the final, it doesn't matter.
—One, but he gets 3 credits for it.
—If you don't know, you can always drop the class before the final.
- How many graduate students does it take to screw in a lightbulb?
—One, but it takes three professors to claim the credit.
- How many doctoral students does it take to screw in a lightbulb?
—I'm writing my dissertation on that very topic; I should have an answer for you in about 5 years.
- How many post-docs does it take to screw in a lightbulb?
—It all depends on the size of the grant.

Merely a Ph.D.

"Your order is confirmed and your credit card has been charged. You have purchased one small liberal-arts college in New England. Thank you for your order."

Christopher Burke

Chapter Three

Shrink Wrap

Hmm... I Wonder What He Meant by That

L.J. Kopf

A wealthy gentleman visits a mental institution where he sees a young woman painting. He admires her work and starts talking to her. After enjoying some sparkling and insightful conversation with her, he says, "You do not belong here. You seem perfectly sane to me. I have a lot of influence. Just leave it to me and you'll be out of here in no time."

"Do you promise, sir?" the artist asks. "Because lots of people have promised to help me get out, but no one has ever kept their word."

"You can count on me," he says.

As the man leaves, he is suddenly struck on the back of the head by a flying object. He falls to the floor, stunned. He sees a brick next to him on the ground and looks around. There stands the artist, some fifteen feet away, her arm still extended in a pitching position.

She smiles at him and says, "You won't forget now, will you?"

No, Mr. Walker, you're wrong. As a practicing psychiatrist, I can assure you that life is not a cruel joke.

Robert Gumpertz

A man had been going to a psychiatrist for many years and finally the doctor pronounced him cured of his mental illness. On hearing the news, the ex-patient smiled, shook the doctor's hand, and pulled out a revolver.

"What the hell are you doing?" screamed the shrink.

"Well, Doc, you helped me a whole lot... but now you know too much!"

SHRINK WRAP

CAN I ACCEPT THIS?

MUELLER

Peter Mueller

A motorist gets a flat tire, so he stops, removes the hubcap, removes the lug nuts, and carefully places the nuts into the hubcap. Unfortunately, before he can get the spare tire on, a strong gust of wind blows the hubcap over and the lug nuts roll right down a sewer drain. He's cursing a blue streak when a man's calm voice interrupts his rant.

"Hey mister —relax! Here's what you do. Take one nut from each of the other three wheels and put them on that one. That'll be good enough to get you to the gas station out on Route 10."

Straightening up to thank him for this practical advice, the motorist sees that the guy is standing behind a sturdy metal fence — behind bars, in fact. About twenty yards down the road there's a gate with a sign reading "Washtenaw County Mental Hospital."

Startled, the motorist says, "Hey, that's effin' brilliant! But what's a fellow like you doing in a place like this?"

And the inmate answers, "C'mon, mister, I may be crazy, but I'm not stupid!"

"Look, going to strip clubs just isn't a healthy coping strategy... Those women only *seem* interested in you and your problems because they know you're going to *pay* them."

Loren Fishman

SOMETIMES, FREUD TRIED TO ANALYZE TOO MUCH.

Kevin Pope

During a session, a psychotherapist says to his client:

"Today we're going to try to analyze your Freudian slips. See, a Freudian slip is when you want to say something but you make a funny mistake and say something slightly different. The analysis of such a mistake can uncover some emotions you may be in conflict with, perhaps some bad memories from your childhood, and so on. Have you made any such funny mistakes lately?"

The client thinks a moment, and responds:

"You know, Doc, yeah, I made a funny mistake while talking to my mother. I was eating dinner with her and I wanted her to pass the salad, but instead I said: "You stupid bitch, you ruined my life, I hate you.""

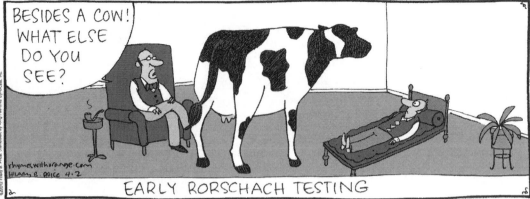

EARLY RORSCHACH TESTING

Hilary Price

A psychoanalyst shows a patient an inkblot, and asks him what he sees. The patient says: "This dude and this chick in bed really going at it, and if you look closely you can see the neighbors listening in through the wall."

The shrink shows him a second inkblot, and the patient says: "That's a lucky guy filming himself in a 3-way with two blonde teenage nymphos."

The psychoanalyst says: "You are obsessed with sex!"

The patient says: "What do you mean *I'm* obsessed? You're the one with all the dirty pictures."

R oses are red
  Violets are blue
    I'm schizophrenic
    And so am I.
        —Oscar Levant

"S chizophrenia beats dining alone."
        —Oscar Levant

T he young man said to the psychiatrist, "I had the oddest dream last night. I dreamt you were my mother. Why on earth would I dream that?"

The psychiatrist said, "Well, let's see… What did you do after having the dream?"

"I had this appointment with you first thing in the morning. I grabbed a cookie and a Coca-Cola for breakfast and rushed over here."

The psychiatrist frowned. "A cookie and a Coca-Cola? *That* you call a breakfast?"

"RORSCHACH! WHAT'S TO BECOME OF YOU?"

Sidney Harris

Shrink Wrap

Joe was seeing a psychoanalyst because at the age of 28 he still believed he had monsters under his bed. It had been years since he had gotten a good night's sleep. But despite the analyst's help, his progress was very poor, and he knew it. One day he stopped seeing the psychoanalyst and decided to try something different.

A few weeks later, Joe met his former analyst in the supermarket. The shrink was surprised to find Joe looking well-rested, energetic, and cheerful. "Doc!" Joe said, "It's amazing! I'm cured!"

"That's great news!" the psychoanalyst said. "You do seem to be doing much better. How?"

"I went to see another doctor," Joe said enthusiastically, "and he cured me in just *one* session!"

"One!?" the psychoanalyst asked incredulously.

"Yeah," continued Joe, "my new doctor is a behaviorist."

"A behaviorist?" the psychoanalyst asked. "How did he cure you in a single session!?"

"Oh, easy," said Joe. "He told me to cut the legs off my bed."

Dan Piraro

During a tour of the mental asylum, a visitor asks the director how they decide whether or not a patient should be institutionalized.

"Well," says the director, "we fill up a bathtub, then we offer a teaspoon, a teacup and a bucket to the patient and ask them to empty the bathtub."

"Oh, I understand," says the visitor. "A normal person would use the bucket because it's bigger than the spoon or the teacup."

"No," says the director, "a normal person would pull the plug. Do you want a bed near a window?"

Insanity: Doing the same thing over and over again and expecting different results.
—Albert Einstein

Dan Piraro

Donald Reilly

Two psychiatrists walking in opposite directions pass each other on the sidewalk, smile, say "Hello," and continue along on their way.

About a half-block later, each one stops, rubs his head, thinks for a moment, then says to himself, "Hmm, I wonder what he meant by that?"

Two behaviorists have just finished having sex. One turns to the other and says "Was that as good for me as it was for you?"

Mrs. Jones, deeply troubled, consults a psychiatrist.

"My husband," she says, "is convinced he's a chicken. He goes around squawking constantly and sleeps on a tiny wood platform up near the ceiling."

"I see," says the psychiatrist thoughtfully. "And how long has your husband been suffering from this fixation?"

"For nearly two years now."

The psychiatrist frowns slightly and asks, "But why have you waited till now to seek help?"

Mrs. Jones blushes and explains, "Well, it was just so nice having a steady supply of eggs."

It was the end of a typically hot, humid, completely miserable New York summer afternoon. Two psychiatrists, coming down in the elevator, their day's work done, were a study in contrasts.

The younger man was utterly wilted and worn out. His hair was rumpled, his clothing wrinkled, his face drained of color. The older man was natty and completely at ease, from the part in his hair, through the starch in his collar, to his confident smile.

The younger man said, "For heaven's sake, Dr. Saperstein, how do you manage it? On a hot day like this, how do you end up so cool?"

"With air conditioning..." began Saperstein.

"I have air conditioning, too," interrupted the younger psychiatrist, "but the patients seem to bring the sultry misery of the New York weather in with them. As I listen to their problems, their eternal whining, their maladjustments, their neuroses, their unhappiness, it's just all too much. It leaves me a wreck. Doesn't listening to all your patients wear you down too?"

"Ah," said Saperstein. "That's the secret. Who listens?"

Shrink Wrap

NORM ACCIDENTALLY GAINS COMPUTER ACCESS TO HIS BRAIN.

Kirk Anderson

The young lady nodded her head at what the psychiatrist was telling her, and said, "Yes, I see, Dr. Schmidt. At least I see everything but one point. The one thing I'm hazy about is the phallic symbol you keep mentioning. What's a phallic symbol?"

"A phallic symbol," says the psychiatrist, "is anything that can be used to represent or symbolize a phallus."

"But what is a phallus, doctor?"

The psychiatrist says, "I think I can explain that most clearly by a demonstration."

He stands up, unzips his fly, and says, "This, my dear young lady, is a phallus."

"Oh," said the lady, suddenly comprehending. "I see. You mean it's like a prick, only smaller."

"I was depressed... I was suicidal; as a matter of fact, I would have killed myself but I was in analysis with a strict Freudian and if you kill yourself they make you pay for the sessions you miss."

—Woody Allen

Vacationer's postcard to his psychiatrist:

Dear Dr. Lipovsky,

Having a great time. Wish you were here to tell me why.

Your client,

Marvin Loewenthal

A very timid guy goes into a bar and sees an attractive woman sitting nearby. It takes him an eternity to gather up his courage, but eventually he goes over to her and mutters a shy hello.

She responds by yelling, at the top of her lungs, "NO! For the last time, I won't sleep with you!"

Everyone in the bar is now staring at them. He slinks back to his table.

A while later, the woman walks over to him, smiles sweetly, and apologizes. "I'm so sorry if I embarrassed you. You see, I'm a graduate student in psychology, and I'm studying how people respond to embarrassing situations."

To which he responds, at the top of *his* lungs, "A hundred dollars?? You only charged those other guys twenty-five!"

Doug Savage

THEN SHE SAID, "MY, WHAT A BIG NOSE YOU HAVE." CAN YOU IMAGINE? I MEAN, DO I HAVE A BIG NOSE? IT'S AVERAGE, RIGHT? AND HOW ABOUT MY EARS? SHE ALSO MENTIONED MY EARS...

offthemark.com   ATLANTIC FEATURE © 1994 MARK PARISI

Mark Parisi

The governor was inspecting the brand-new state psychiatric hospital and on being taken through the isolation wards was surprised to see that in one cell sat a man of distinguished demeanor, reading a copy of the Wall Street Journal, and wearing nothing but a silk top hat.

Seeing the governor and his entourage, the inmate rose, bowed politely, and said in cultured tones, "Sir, I perceive you are a man of importance and it strikes me that you must be curious as to why I sit here in the nude."

"Well, yes," said the governor cautiously. "The thought had indeed struck me."

"It's not at all mysterious," said the inmate. "The cell is air-conditioned, as you will note, and is maintained at a most comfortable temperature, and this is after all the isolation ward. Since clothing is not necessary either for warmth, modesty, or adornment, why bother with it at all?"

"True," muttered the governor. "But tell me," he said, "in that case, why the top hat?"

The inmate shrugged. "Oh, well, someone might come."

Welcome to the Psychiatric Hotline. Please listen carefully because some of our options have changed:

- If you are obsessive-compulsive, press 1 repeatedly.
- If you are co-dependent, please ask someone to press 2 for you.
- If you have multiple personalities, press 3, 4, 5, and 6.
- If you are paranoid, we already know who you are and what you want. Just stay on the line so we can trace your call.
- If you are delusional, press 7 and your call will be transferred to the mothership.
- If you are schizophrenic, listen carefully and a small voice will tell you which number to press.
- If you are depressed, it doesn't matter which number you press. No one will answer.
- If you have amnesia, press 8 and state your name, address, phone number, date of birth, social security number, and your mother's maiden name.
- If you have low self-esteem, please hang up. None of our operators have the slightest interest in speaking with you.
- If you have short-term memory loss, press 9. If you have short-term memory loss, press 9. If you have short-term memory loss, press 9. If you have short-term memory loss, press 9...

I don't go to my psychiatrist anymore. He was meddling too much in my private life.

You ought to meet my psychiatrist. He's wonderful. He always finds something wrong with you.

The psychiatrist said to the comedian, "Lie down and tell me everything you know." He did, and now the psychiatrist is in Chicago doing the comic's act.

Psychiatric Advice

Doctor, doctor, I keep thinking I'm a pair of curtains!
—Pull yourself together, man!

Doctor, doctor, I keep thinking I'm a bell.
—Well, just go home and if the feeling persists, give me a ring.

Doctor, doctor, my sister thinks she's an elevator.
—Tell her to come right in.
—I can't. She doesn't stop at this floor.

Doctor, doctor, nobody understands me.
—What do you mean by that?

Doctor, doctor, people keep ignoring me!
—Next!

Doctor, doctor, no one believes a word I say.
—Tell me the truth now, what's your *real* problem?

Doctor, doctor, I feel like a pack of cards.
—I'll deal with you later.

Doctor, doctor, people keep telling me I'm ugly!
—Lie on the couch. Face down!

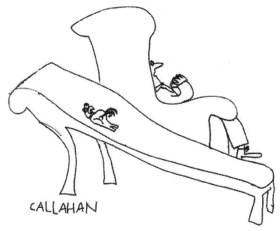

"Do you need a cracker, or do you just want a cracker?

John Callahan

Doctor, Doctor, I can't stop stealing things.
—Take these pills for a week. If that doesn't work, I'll take a new iPad!

Doctor, doctor, I've only got 59 seconds to live.
—Just a minute, please.

Leo Cullum

Mark Stivers

A guy enters his psychiatrist's office wearing nothing but ski boots, silver body paint, and a top hat and monocle. A myna bird is perched on his shoulder and a tv antenna protrudes from the top hat. He says to the shrink: "Doc, I really gotta talk to you about my brother."

"If you can't get rid of the skeleton in your closet, you'd best teach it to dance."
—George Bernard Shaw

I went into a bookstore today and asked where the self-help section was. The saleswoman said, "If I told you, that would defeat the whole purpose."

There's nothing wrong with the average person that a good psychiatrist can't exaggerate.

In Hollywood, if you don't have a psychiatrist, people think you're crazy.

Nature? Nurture? Either way, it's your parent's fault.

"Psychiatry enables us to correct our faults by confessing our parents' shortcomings."
—Laurence J. Peter

Did you hear about the auto mechanic who went to a psychiatrist?
—He insisted on lying under the couch.

Did you hear about the psycho-analyst who used to be an interior decorator?
—She was the only shrink in town with Freudian slip covers.

Sidney Harris

Shrink Wrap

"I'm not on YouTube."

© MARK ANDERSON WWW.ANDERTOONS.COM

Mark Anderson

Why did the behavioralist cross the road?

—It doesn't matter.

"Okay, I admit it, I do have a multiple personality disorder," said Tom, being perfectly frank.

• "I've stopped seeing my therapist," said Tom unshrinkingly.

How many therapists does it take to screw in a lightbulb?

—Just one, but it takes fifteen visits.

• How many psychoanalysts does it take to screw in a lightbulb?

—How many do you think it takes?

• How many psychiatrists does it take to change a lightbulb?

—Only one, but the lightbulb has to really want to change.

• How many Freudians does it take to screw in a lightbulb?

—Two. One to hold the bulb and the other to hold his penis... I mean ladder... I meant to say ladder.

Chapter Four

Is It Art Yet?

The Painter Crosses the Road

Paul Soderblom

Mark Parisi

Why did the painter cross the road?
    —To see from the other side.

The "earth" without "art" is just "eh."

And the first rude sketch that the
    world had seen
        Was joy to his mighty heart,
        Till the Devil whispered behind the
        leaves
        "It's pretty, but is it Art?"
            —Rudyard Kipling

Dan Piraro

"Art is art. Everything else is everything else."
—Ad Reinhardt

"Well, art is art, isn't it? Still, on the other hand, water is water. And east is east and west is west, and if you take cranberries and stew them like applesauce they taste much more like prunes than rhubarb does. Now you tell me what you know."
—Groucho Marx

Dan Piraro

"Life imitates art far more than art imitates life."
—Oscar Wilde

"Life doesn't imitate art, it imitates bad television."
—Woody Allen

"I choose a block of marble and chop off whatever I don't need."
—Auguste Rodin

Calvin and Hobbes

CALVIN AND HOBBES © 1992 Watterson. Reprinted with permission of UNIVERSAL UCLICK. All rights reserved.

Bill Watterson

Every day the anxious painter had been asking the owner of the gallery where he was exhibiting if any of his work had sold, but every day the answer was no.

That is, until the day the gallery owner was able to tell him, "Well, today there's good news and there's bad news."

The painter asks to hear the good news first. "So this gentleman came in, took a quick look at your work, and asked me if you were a good painter. I said yes indeed. He asked if your work would live on, and I said without a doubt. Finally he asked if your work would become more valuable after your death. When I told him I was sure it would, he bought everything you had in the gallery at top price."

The painter says, "Awesome! ...but what's the bad news?"

"He was your doctor."

In Paris in the 1920s, a decidedly bohemian young lady not surprisingly found herself attracted to an up-and-coming avant-garde artist. She succeeded in attaching herself to him, but the affair lasted only a month.

"All his weirdness is in his work," she complained.

ARTIST TO CRITIC: So what's your opinion of my painting?

CRITIC: It's worthless.

ARTIST: I know, but I'd like to hear it anyway.

"The critic has to educate the public; the artist has to educate the critic."
—Oscar Wilde

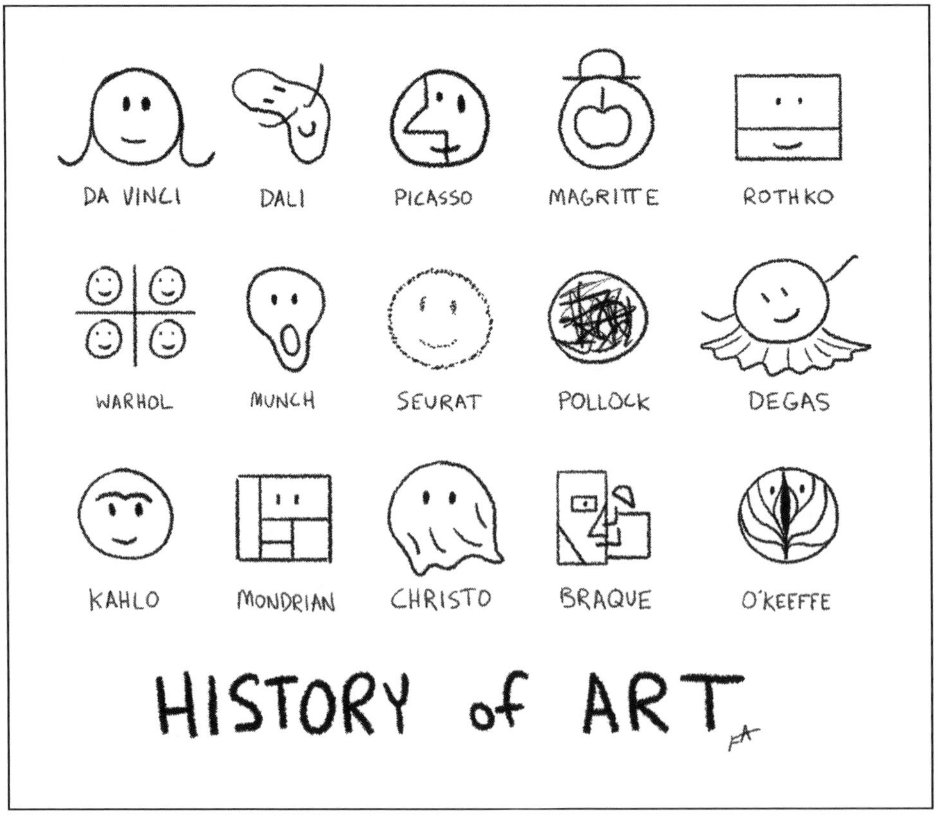
DA VINCI
DALI
PICASSO
MAGRITTE
ROTHKO
WARHOL
MUNCH
SEURAT
POLLOCK
DEGAS
KAHLO
MONDRIAN
CHRISTO
BRAQUE
O'KEEFFE
HISTORY of ART
FA

Francis Acupan

Mark Stivers

You just might be an artist if ...

...the only piece of new furniture you have in your home is a $900 easel.

...you've ever cleaned your fingernails with a palette knife.

...you butter your toast with your fingers, just to feel its texture.

...you've ever considered framing your palette instead of the painting.

...you know the difference between beige, ecru, cream, off-white, and eggshell.

...you notice the burnt umber in the background of the *Playboy* centerfold.

...your three children are forced to share a room so you can have an art studio.

...you carry pencils instead of pens.

...you never look at a person's face as a whole, instead breaking it up into lines and shadows and shapes.

...the suggestion that you should get a job in advertising or go to law school makes you want to scream and throw things.

...you are over fifty and still have no health insurance.

...you totally judge a book by its cover.

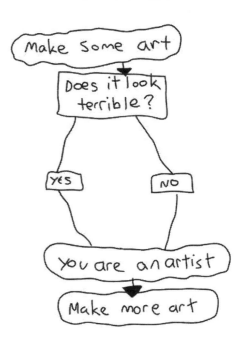

"What did Jesus order?"

Leo Cullum

After a two-year visit to the United States, Michelangelo's "David" is returning to Italy .

W hat did Christ say at the Last Supper?

—"Why don't we all come and sit on this side of the table?"

Is It Art Yet?

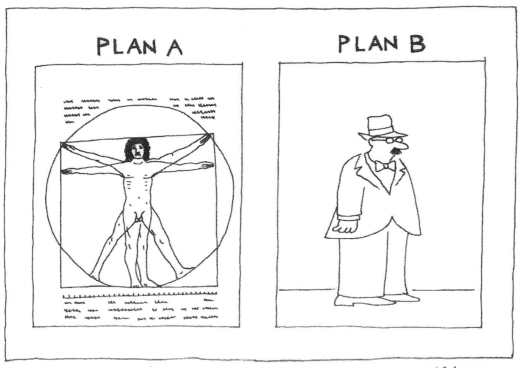

PLAN A   PLAN B

Mick Stevens

Jeff Hobbs

Bradford Veley

A highly successful art dealer is walking along Madison Avenue when he notices a nasty, mangy cat lapping milk from a saucer in the doorway of a grocer's.

He does a double-take.

He sees that the saucer is not just an old dish, but is in fact a rare and very valuable piece of Ming Dynasty porcelain. Casually he walks into the grocery store and offers to buy the cat for twenty bucks.

The store owner replies, "I'm sorry, but the cat isn't for sale."

The collector says, "Please, I need a cat around the house to catch rodents. The situation is out of control and my wife is threatening to leave me. Hell, I'll give you $200 for the cat."

And the owner says "Sold," and hands over the cat.

The collector slyly continues, "Hey, for the two hundred bucks I wonder if you could throw in that old saucer. The cat's used to it and it'll save me from having to get a dish."

The owner says, "Sorry, but that's my lucky saucer. So far this week I've sold thirty cats."

"It is only an auctioneer who can equally and impartially admire all schools of art."
—Oscar Wilde

Said to be a true story: An art dealer bought a canvas signed by 'Picasso' and travelled all the way to Cannes to discover whether or not it was genuine. Picasso was working in his studio. He cast a single look at the canvas and said, "It's a fake."

A few months later, the dealer bought another canvas signed 'Picasso'. Again he travelled to Cannes, and again Picasso, after a single glance, grunted: "It's a fake."

"But cher maître," insisted the dealer, "it so happens that I saw you with my own eyes working on this very picture several years ago."

Picasso shrugged: "I often paint fakes."

"ON SOME OF THE PAINTINGS MY RIGHT BRAIN SAYS THEY'RE GOOD ART, BUT MY LEFT BRAIN SAYS THEY'RE BAD INVESTMENTS. ON OTHERS, MY RIGHT BRAIN SAYS THEY'RE BAD ART, BUT MY LEFT BRAIN SAYS THEY'RE GOOD INVESTMENTS."

Sidney Harris

"**B**ad artists copy, great artists steal."
—Picasso

"**O**riginality is the fine art of remembering what you hear but forgetting where you heard it."
—Laurence J. Peter

Two well-heeled ladies pay their first visit ever to the Metropolitan Museum of Art. In one of the 19th-century rooms they come across a beautiful oil painting of a ragged but jolly vagabond. Says one lady to the other, "Sure, he's too broke to buy a decent suit of clothes, but he can afford to get his portrait painted!"

"Then what happened?"

Barney Tobey

Andy Singer

D efinition of modern art =
I could do that +
Yeah, but you didn't.

"I t is not hard to understand
modern art. If it hangs on
a wall it's a painting, and
if you can walk around it
it's a sculpture."
—Tom Stoppard

The Worst Date Ever

Rob Murray

Is It Art Yet?

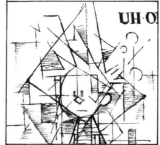

CALVIN AND HOBBES © 1990 Watterson. Reprinted with permission of UNIVERSAL UCLICK. All rights reserved.

Bill Watterson

M AN RAY: A man in love with a woman from a different era. I see a photograph!

LUIS BUÑUEL: I see a film!

GIL: I see insurmountable problem!

SALVADOR DALI: I see rhinoceros!

—Woody Allen, *Midnight in Paris*

"L ast year I went fishing with Salvador Dali. He was using a dotted line. He caught every other fish."

   —Steven Wright

A wealthy man commissioned Pablo Picasso to paint a portrait of his wife. Startled by the non-representational image on the final canvas, the husband complained, "It isn't how she really looks."

Asked how she really looked, the man produced a photograph from his wallet. Returning the photograph, Picasso observed, "Small, isn't she?"

WHILE SOME STILL PREFERRED TO WALK THE MUSEUM, THE ZIP LINE TOUR ATTRACTED A WHOLE NEW CLIENTELE.

Hilary Price

"A painting in a museum hears more ridiculous opinions than anything else in the world."
—Edmond de Goncourt

"Murals in restaurants are on a par with the food in museums."
—Peter De Vries

"What would I put in a museum? Probably a museum! That's an amusing relic of our past."
—John Hodgman

"Which painting in the National Gallery would I save if there was a fire? The one nearest the door, of course."
—George Bernard Shaw

"I went to a museum where they had all the heads and arms for the statues from the other museums... One time I went to a museum where all the work in the museum had been done by children. They had all the paintings up on refrigerators."
—Steven Wright

A man goes into a museum and accidentally breaks a statue.

The museum guard says to him, "That's a 500-year-old piece you just broke."

The man answers, "Phew! Thank God it's not a new one."

A thief in Paris hatched a plan to steal several celebrated paintings from the Louvre in the middle of the night. Thanks to some very meticulous preparations, he was able to slip past security, steal the paintings, and get them safely into his van. However, he was captured only two blocks away when his van ran out of gas.

When asked how he could mastermind such a crime and then make such an obvious error, he replied, "Monsieur, that is why I stole the paintings. I had no Monet to buy Degas to make the Van Gogh so I knew I had nothing Toulouse."

I visited the Louvre Museum in Paris last month. I asked if it was okay to take a picture and they said it was. I must say, the Mona Lisa looks pretty damn good hanging on my living room wall.

Is It Art Yet?

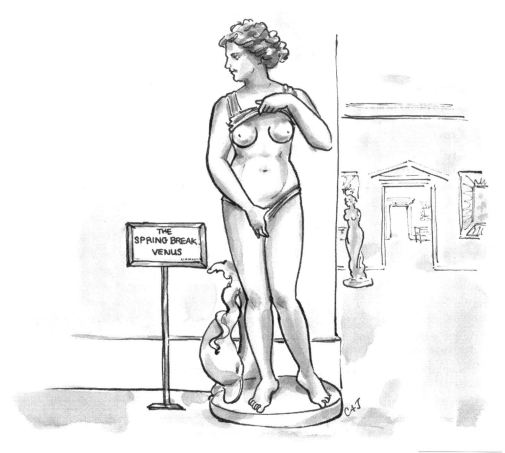

Carolita Johnson

MUSEUM GUARD BOB ABRAHAMS BEGINS TO SUSPECT SOMEONE'S BEEN MESSING WITH THE AUDIO TOUR TAPES

Dan Piraro

Calvin and Hobbes

YOU KNOW HOW PEOPLE LOOK AT MODERN ART AND ALWAYS SAY, "MY 6-YEAR-OLD KID COULD DO THAT!"?

WELL, THAT GAVE ME THIS GREAT IDEA! I'VE DECIDED TO BECOME A FORGER AND GET RICH PASSING OFF FAKE PAINTINGS TO MUSEUMS!

A LOT OF PAINTINGS SELL FOR TENS OF MILLIONS OF DOLLARS NOW, SO I MAKE A PRETTY GOOD HOURLY RATE.

YOU SHOULD PROBABLY SCRATCH OUT THE COPYRIGHT DATE ON THE CARTOON STATIONERY.

OOH YEAH, GLAD YOU CAUGHT THAT!

CALVIN AND HOBBES © 1993 Watterson. Reprinted with permission of UNIVERSAL UCLICK. All rights reserved.

Bill Watterson

There was an artist who worked from a studio in his home. He specialized in nudes, and had been working with the same model for a long period of time. On this particular day, his model showed up at the usual time and, after exchanging the usual small talk, began to disrobe for the day's work.

The artist suddenly began to feel a bit under the weather, and told her not to bother, explaining that he sensed a bad cold coming on. He insisted that he would pay her for the day anyway, and that she could just go home. All he wanted to do was relax with some hot tea with lemon and honey.

The model said, "Oh, please, let me fix it for you. It's the least I can do."

He agreed, and told her to fix herself a cup as well. They were sitting in the living room chatting and enjoying their tea, when he heard the front door open and close, and then some familiar footsteps.

"Oh my!" he whispered, "My wife is back early! Quick —take your clothes off!!"

Mrs. Gladstone instructed the artist painting her portrait to add to it a gold bracelet on each of her wrists, a strand of pearls around her neck, ruby earrings, and a diamond tiara.

The artist pointed out that this would be tantamount to lying.

Said the lady, "Look, my husband's running around with a young blonde. After I die, I want her to go crazy looking for the jewelry."

Is It Art Yet?

Harry Bliss

Bradford Veley

Dan Piraro

"I don't think you're supposed to like it."

David Sipress

A distinguished Soviet aesthetician was answering questions on the theory of art.

"What is expressionism?" one questioner asked.

"Expressionism is painting what you feel."

"What is impressionism?"

"Impressionism is painting what you see."

"And what is socialist realism?"

"Socialist realism is painting what you hear."

In the lobby of a Moscow hotel across from a Russian Orthodox Monastery:

"You are welcome to visit the cemetery where famous Russian and Soviet composers, artists, and writers are buried daily except Thursday."

"They couldn't find the artist so they hung the picture."
—Frank Zappa

"Art is what you can get away with."
—Andy Warhol

"Crazy is a term of art; *insane* is a term of law. Remember that, and you will save yourself a lot of trouble."
—Hunter S. Thompson

"*Escher! Get your ass up here.*"

Robert Leighton

"Only those who attempt the absurd will achieve the impossible... I think it's in my basement, let me go upstairs and check."
—M.C. Escher

Hilary Price

Two nude statues in a Paris park, one of the stunningly handsome Adonis, the other of the ravishingly gorgeous Venus, have been gazing longingly at each other across a pathway for exactly one hundred years, when an angel comes down from Heaven. With a single wave of her hand, the angel brings the two to life. "As a reward for being so patient through a century of scorching summers and brutal winters," proclaims the angel, "you have both been given life for thirty minutes to do whatever you'd like the most."

The statues exchange radiant smiles, and with meaningful looks they quickly go running behind the shrubbery. The angel waits approvingly as the bushes rustle, giggling and panting are heard, and perhaps the earth shakes a little. After fifteen minutes, the two return, out of breath and laughing.

The angel tells them, "Um, you have fifteen minutes left. Would you care to do it again?"

He asks her, "Shall we, my love?"

She eagerly replies, "Oh, yes, dearest, let's! But let's change positions. This time, I'll hold the pigeon down and you crap on its head."

Hilary Price

Is It Art Yet?

Dave Coverly

Walking home from the pub last night, I passed ten men in an alleyway holding knives, all poised to stab me.

When I looked again, I realized it was actually a sculpture consisting of shapes carved on the wall in such a manner as to stand out from the surrounding background.

That sure was a massive relief.

I think I may be a talented photographer. I took just one photo with my camera phone and it asked me if I wanted to open a gallery.

I don't do jokes about graphic designers. I draw the line at that.

What's the difference between San Jose and yogurt?
    —Yogurt has culture.

What did blue say to orange?
    —Why can't you accept a complement?

Before Instagram

Flash Rosenberg

"This is the Venus de Milo," the museum guard said disarmingly.

• "I'm not leaving the chapel until I finish this painting," Michelangelo insisted.

• "I'm tired of smiling," moaned Lisa.

• "Now I can do some painting," said Tom easily.

• "I know you won't take my advice, Mr. Van Gogh, but you should quit painting and get a real job," said Tom unconvincingly.

• "I prefer Pollock," Jack's son expressed, abstractly.

How many dadaists does it take to screw in a lightbulb?
 —Fish.

• How many surrealists does it take to screw in a lightbulb?
 —Two: One to walk the fish and the other to listen to it growing.

• How many contemporary artists does it take to screw in a lightbulb?
 —Four. One to throw bulbs against the wall, one to pile hundreds of them in a heap and spray-paint them orange, one to glue the lightbulbs to a cocker spaniel, and one to put a bulb in the socket and fill the room with light while all the critics and buyers are watching the fellow smashing the bulbs against the wall, the fellow with the spray-gun, and the cocker spaniel.

Chapter Five

What, and Quit Show Business?

Getting to Carnegie Hall

"Of course, what I'd really like to do is direct."

Mort Gerberg

"It is a hopeless endeavour to attract people to a theatre unless they can be first brought to believe that they will never get in."
—Charles Dickens

"Never fear to take your curtain call to the sound of one hand clapping."
—Charles Ludlam

PHILIP HENSLOWE: Mr. Fennyman, allow me to explain about the theatre business. The natural condition is one of insurmountable obstacles on the road to imminent disaster.
HUGH FENNYMAN: So what do we do?
PHILIP HENSLOWE: Nothing. Strangely enough, it all turns out well.
HUGH FENNYMAN: How?
PHILIP HENSLOWE: I don't know. It's a mystery.
—*Shakespeare in Love* (Marc Norman & Tom Stoppard)

If all the world is a stage, where is the audience sitting?

IRA (A CRITIC): I don't understand you people. One minute you're at each other's throats, and the next, you want to do another play together.
JAMES (AN ACTOR): It's theater. What don't you understand?
—Terrence McNally, *It's Only a Play*

"The play was a great success, but the audience was a disaster."
—Oscar Wilde

George Bernard Shaw once sent two tickets to the opening night of one of his plays to Winston Churchill, along with the message, "Dear Winston: Here are two tickets for yourself and a friend, assuming you have a friend."

Churchill returned the tickets with the note, "Dear Bernard: A prior engagement prevents my attending opening night. Please replace these with tickets for the second night, assuming there is a second night."

"I thought I loved it, but Gordon said we were just manipulated."

Willliam Hamilton

Jules Feiffer

"One of the first and most important things for a critic to learn is how to sleep undetected at the theatre."
—William Archer

"A critic is a man who knows the way but can't drive the car."
—Kenneth Tynan

"Critics are like eunuchs in a harem; they know how it's done, they've seen it done every day, but they're unable to do it themselves."
—Brendan Behan

"I love criticism just so long as it's unqualified praise."
—Noel Coward

"Ultimately one has to pity these poor souls who know every secret about writing, directing, designing, producing, and acting but are stuck in those miserable day jobs writing reviews. Will somebody help them, please?"
—David Ives

THEATER ON MEDS

MUELLER

Peter Mueller

What, and Quit Show Business?

"Aeschylus is good, I suppose, but I go to the theatre to relax."

James Stevenson

A professor of classical theatre takes his torn suit to a Greek tailor. The tailor looks at the pants and says, "Euripides?"

"Yes," replies the professor, "Euminides?"

"I once had a girl, or should I say, she once had me..."

—Oedipus Rex

Miss Smith had read through *Hamlet* for the first time and was asked her opinion of it.

"Really," she said, "I don't know why people rave about it. It's nothing but a bunch of quotations strung together."

"The remarkable thing about Shakespeare is that he really is very good, in spite of all the people who say he is very good."

—Robert Graves

"The most stringent protection of free speech would not protect a man in falsely shouting fire in a theatre and causing a panic."

—Supreme Court Justice Oliver Wendell Holmes, Jr. (Schenck v. United States; 3 March 1919)

Rosencrantz leaps up and bellows at the audience:
ROSENCRANTZ: Fire!
Guildenstern: Where?
ROSENCRANTZ: It's all right —I'm demonstrating the misuse of free speech. To prove that it exists.
He regards the audience with contempt.
Not a move. They should burn to death in their shoes.

—Tom Stoppard, *Rosencrantz & Guildenstern Are Dead*

THE GLOBE THEATRE, 1601

"The following play contains scenes of treachery, fratricide and indecision, which some viewers may find upsetting..."

Rob Murray

Yiddish-speaking cab driver taking John Barrymore uptown to star in *Hamlet* on Broadway: "You think it'll play in English?"

QUOTE: "To be or not to be; that is the question. Whether 'tis nobler in the mind to suffer the slings and arrows of outrageous fortune..."

ANAGRAM: "In one of the Bard's best-thought-of tragedies, our insistent hero, Hamlet, queries on two fronts about how life turns rotten."

"I know not, sir, whether Bacon wrote the works of Shakespeare, but if he did not, it seems to me that he missed the opportunity of a lifetime."

— James Barrie

JENKINS: The plays of Shakespeare were, in fact, never written by Shakespeare.

HELGA: Really?

JENKINS: They were written by another playwright of the same name!

***

EDMUND: Shakespeare wrote shameless potboilers. That's why he called them *As You Like It*, *Much Ado About Nothing*, and *What You Will*...

STONE: Are you denying the genius of Shakespeare?

EDMUND: No, I am only saying that in the theatre, genius is often wedded to a mountebank.

—Charles Ludlam, *Stage Blood*

Dave Coverly

What, and Quit Show Business?

"Look, just finish college, get your MBA, have a career, and then
if you want to try your hand at acting, you'll have my blessing."

Robert Mankoff

A little boy says to his mother, "Mommy, when I grow up I wanna be an actor!" "Well, honey," she explains, "you know you can't do both."

A television celebrity, determined to prove himself an actor, had undertaken the role of Hamlet in a regional theatre production. Not surprisingly, he was abysmal. So abysmal, in fact, that a few lines into the "To be or not to be..." soliloquy the audience began to boo loudly.

Unaccustomed to such treatment, our star dropped character, stepped downstage, and told the audience, "Don't blame me. I didn't write this crap!"

"We used to have actors trying to become celebrities. Now we have celebrities trying to become actors."
—Laurence Olivier

"Acting is all about honesty. If you can fake that, you've got it made."
—George Burns

Laurence Olivier on the set of *Marathon Man*, seeing Dustin Hoffman, who had not slept for three days in order to better inhabit his character: "My dear boy, why don't you try acting?"

"Just know your lines and don't bump into the furniture."
—Noel Coward

"We're actors. We're the opposite of people!"
—Tom Stoppard, *Rosencrantz & Guildenstern Are Dead*

"It's one of the tragic ironies of the theatre that only one man in it can count on steady work: the night watchman."
—Tallulah Bankhead

What, and Quit Show Business?

For four decades, Lynn Fontane and Alfred Lunt were the reigning King and Queen of Broadway, a married couple who co-starred in a slew of successful productions. In fact, between 1928 and their retirement in 1960, the couple never appeared on stage separately.

Late in her career, an interviewer was speaking to Fontane about this long, enduring partnership and the difficulties of husband and wife working together so intimately for so long. She asked Fontane, "Didn't you ever consider divorce?"

Fontane replied: "Divorce, never. Murder, many times."

BREAKDOWN OF NEW YORK CITY THEATRE FRATERNITIES:

The Lambs are a bunch of actors pretending to be gentlemen.

The Players are a bunch of gentlemen pretending to be actors.

And the Friars are neither, pretending to be both.

RESPECT THE TECH

- LIGHTING: I gave you light. The least you can do is stand in it.
- COSTUMES: You might lie but the tape measure won't.
- SOUND: It'a microphone, not a miracle.
- PROPS: If it's not yours, don't touch it.
- TD: I built it like you drew it.
- CREW: If we're not happy, you won't be either.
- DESIGNER: Fast, cheap, good. Choose any two.
- STAGE MANAGER: "Warning" is not a suggestion. "Places" is not a category on Jeopardy. "Go" is not an option.
- DIRECTOR:
  1. Leave your ego at the door.
  2. Get off book.
  3. Do more and talk less.
  4. Repeat steps 1thru 3.

YOU KNOW YOU WORK IN NOT-FOR-PROFIT THEATRE IF...

...your living room sofa spends more time on stage than you do.

...you have your own secret recipe for stage blood.

...you can find a prop in the prop room that hasn't seen the light of day in ten years, but you don't know where your own vacuum cleaner is.

...you start buying your work clothes at Goodwill so you can buy your costumes at Bloomingdale's.

...you've scheduled your vacation time to coincide with tech week.

...you've ever cleaned a tuxedo with a magic marker.

..you've ever gotten a part because you were the only one who fit the costume.

...you've ever gotten a part because you were the only one who showed up to audition.

...you are recognized the minute you walk on stage because the audience saw you taking out the trash before the show.

...you've ever had to haul a sofa off stage between scenes wearing an evening gown and heels.

...you've ever had to haul a sofa off stage between scenes wearing an evening gown and heels — and you're a guy.

...you've ever said "Just paint it black — no one will ever see it."

...you've ever had to play a drunk scene opposite someone who really was drunk.

...you've ever said "Don't worry, here's some duct tape. If that doesn't work, we'll just hot-glue it."

What Hollywood Teaches Us

- Natural disasters, alien attacks, and zombie uprisings only happen in the United States. Thank God the rest of the world is safe!

- The United States military and police are useless. The country can only be saved by Ironman, Spiderman, Superman, or the Avengers.

- When a science experiment goes wrong, it always produces either a superhero or a supervillain.

- It does not matter if you are Spiderman or Batman. Your girlfriend will always find a reason to dump you.

- No matter who you are, whatever you do, wherever you hide, Liam Neeson will find you and kill you.

- Bullets miraculously just miss the good guys —even from a machine gun.

- Five-year-old girls and boys have an uncanny ability to communicate with evil spirits.

- Whenever there's a car chase, the first people who should be notified are owners of sidewalk fruit stands.

- If staying in a haunted house, women should investigate any strange noises in their most revealing underwear.

- No matter how poor you are, you can always afford a spiffy new suit and tie.

- Ancient Romans had English accents and their armor never got dirty

- If you know karate or kung fu, every villain you run into will also be a black belt.

- You can always find a woman to go home with you by buying her a drink at the bar.

- The probability of getting laid as a high school student in the U.S. is 600% higher than as an engineering student in India.

- Every American sitting in a plush Manhattan office works 18 hours a day but still finds time to remain gym-toned.

- All romances start with both people not being able to stand each other.

- Madonna is 55 and her boyfriend is 22. JLo is 42 & her boyfriend is 26. Don't worry teens, your boyfriend hasn't been born yet.

- That odd-looking, ill-mannered black dude will turn out to be a real prince of a guy in the end.

- India is all about cows and traffic.

- There are two types of Indians: one's a thermonuclear physicist, the other is "the funny guy."

- Wherever you go in India some random sitar music will start playing.

- What Africans?

"Strip away the phony tinsel of Hollywood and you'll find the real tinsel underneath."
　　　—Oscar Levant

"My last picture for Warners was *Romance on the High Seas*. It was Doris Day's first picture; that was before she became a virgin."
　　　—Oscar Levant

GARY: Andy my honey, Andy my multi-talented, prime-time delight. You don't do art. You buy it... You're better than that. An actor, what, that's just some English guy who can't get a series... *Hamlet*. Andy, I have to say this, 'cause we're buds, and I cherish that budship —but think reputation. Word on the street. When folks —let's call 'em Hollywood— when they hear you're doing the greatest play in the English-speaking world, they're gonna know you're washed up!
—Paul Rudnick, *I Hate Hamlet*

An agent calls up a producer and says, "Watch out! There's a man at your door this very minute, and he's got a gun and says he's going to kill you. But actually, that isn't what I called about."

Calvin and Hobbes

ANOTHER THING TO REMEMBER ABOUT POPULAR CULTURE IS THAT TODAY'S TV-REARED AUDIENCE IS HIP AND SOPHISTICATED. THIS STUFF DOESN'T AFFECT US.

WE CAN SEPARATE FACT FROM FICTION. WE UNDERSTAND SATIRE AND IRONY. WE'RE DETACHED AND JADED VIEWERS WHO AREN'T INFLUENCED BY WHAT WE WATCH.

I THINK I HEAR ADVERTISERS LAUGHING.

HOLD ON, I NEED TO INFLATE MY BASKETBALL SHOES.

CALVIN AND HOBBES © 1995 Watterson. Reprinted with permission of UNIVERSAL UCLICK. All rights reserved.

Bill Watterson

An actor comes home one evening to find his bedroom in disarray, the floor strewn with torn garments, and his wife naked on the bed, trying to catch her breath. Outside the window some guy is making his escape down the drainpipe.

He tells her menacingly, "You'd better have a really good explanation for all this."

She gasps, "Your agent just dropped by. I don't know what came over me, but I tore off his clothes and ravished him."

"My agent? Huh... Listen, did he say anything about the Paramount deal?"

Satan visits a film producer and offers her a deal: "I'll guarantee that your next film is a billion-dollar-grossing, sequel-spawning, blockbuster hit. All I require in return is that your husband's soul, your children's souls, and THEIR children's souls must rot in Hell for eternity."

The producer thinks for a moment and says, "What's the catch?"

"It's worse than dog eats dog. It's dog doesn't return dog's phone calls."
    —Woody Allen

When the great director Orson Welles passed away, he went straight to Heaven. He was warmly greeted by St. Peter, who wasted no time in asking him to make one more film. "I'm tired," said Welles. "I just want to rest."

"But this will be one for the ages," insisted Saint Peter. "We've got Shakespeare writing the screenplay, DaVinci designing the sets, and Beethoven composing the score."

"Wow!!" said Welles. "Really?"

"Really."

"In that case, how can I say no?"

"But there's one thing I should warn you about," explained St. Peter. "God does have this girlfriend who thinks she can act..."

"Working on television is like being shot out of a cannon. They cram you all up with rehearsals, then someone lights a fuse and — BANG — there you are in someone's living room."
    —Tallulah Bankhead

"And now, Dr. Wagner and Dr. Avery will demonstrate, through interpretive dance, how inflation in developing nations impacts the formation of global monetary policies!"

Bradford Veley

Why did the dancer cross the road?
—Because she had to do it on the other side.

"Dancing is a perpendicular expression of a horizontal desire."
—George Bernard Shaw

"This particular species is believed to have travelled in troupes."

Joe Dator

98

"Damn it, Persky! I ask you for a fiercely choreographed rite of destruction and rebirth, and you give me a febrile study of dehumanized angst."

Robert Mankoff

A big believer in eugenics, the legendary and stunningly beautiful dancer Isadora Duncan once suggested to the renowned playwright George Bernard Shaw that they should have a child together. "Think of it!" she said. "With your brains and my body, what a wonder it would be."

Without missing a beat, Shaw replied: "Yes, but what if it had my body and your brains?"

Henny Youngman on ballerinas on pointe:
"Why didn't they just hire taller girls?"

"I could dance with you until the cows come home. On second thought, I'd rather dance with the cows until you come home."
—Groucho Marx

I haven't seen choreography that stiff since the Lee Harvey Oswald prison transfer.

How to Twerk:
  Step One: Reconsider.

In an inexplicable attack of nerves, Elliot becomes the first person ever to screw up John Cage's 4'33".

Loren Fishman

A young man on the streets of New York City stops an older gentleman and asks him, "How can I get to Carnegie Hall?"
—"Practice, practice."

An intellectual is someone who can listen to the William Tell Overture without thinking about the Lone Ranger.

I just met a pop music conspiracy theorist. Apparently the moonwalk was faked.

"I worry that the person who thought up Muzak may be thinking up something else."
—Lily Tomlin

"A piano is a piano is a piano."
— Gertrude Steinway

"Writing about music is like dancing about architecture."
—Laurie Anderson

[also: Steve Martin, Frank Zappa, Martin Mull, Elvis Costello, Thelonius Monk, Clara Schumann, Miles Davis, George Carlin]

A young man is said to have approached the renowned composer Wolfgang Amadeus Mozart, clearly one of the great musical prodigies of all time, and asked, "Herr Mozart, I have the great desire to write symphonies. Perhaps you can advise me how to get started."

Mozart said, "The best advice I can give you is to wait until you are older and more experienced, and try your hand at less ambitious pieces to begin with."

The young man was taken aback. "But, Herr Mozart, you yourself wrote ambitious symphonies when you were considerably younger than I."

"Ah," said Mozart, "but I did so without asking advice."

"I understand that the inventor of the bagpipes was inspired when he saw a man carrying an indignant, asthmnatic pig under his arm. Unfortunately, the man-made sound never quite equaled the purity of the sound achieved by the pig."
—Alfred Hitchcock

I'm thinking about selling my theremin. I haven't touched it in years.

"Everybody stand back! I'm an ethnomusicologist."

Loren Fishman

What is the question to which "9W" is the answer?

—Excuse me, Mr. Wagner, but is that spelled with a "V"?

"Wagner's music is better than it sounds."

　　—Bill Nye

"Opera is when a guy gets stabbed in the back and, instead of bleeding, he sings."

　　—Robert Benchley

"People are wrong when they say opera is not what it used to be. It is what it used to be. That is what's wrong with it."

　　—Noel Coward

What did the lecherous conductor say to the curvaceous first violinist?

—Put your Brahms around me, baby, and scratch my Bach.

Knock knock.
　　Who's there?
　　Knock knock.
　　Who's there?
　　Knock knock.
　　Who's there?
　　Knock knock.
　　Who's there?
　　Philip Glass.

PETER (A PLAYWRIGHT): I wrote my first play in high school. The Life of George Gershwin. I got all my information from the back of record jackets. In the first scene, young George got thrown out of a music publisher's office. The secretary consoled him and shyly confessed she was a budding lyricist. "What's your name?" George asked her. "Ira," my first heroine said. I think my career has been downhill ever since.

—Terrence McNally, *It's Only a Play*

Mark Stivers

Dan Piraro

A violinist believes that his music has become so captivating that he can now march into the deepest jungle and use it to tame savage beasts. One day he does just that, and soon two lions are sitting quietly, entranced by the music of Mozart. A panther and a leopard draw close and join the appreciative audience. Suddenly a hyena comes crashing through the underbrush, pounces on the violinist, and devours him.

"Why did you do a thing like that?" one of the lions protests. "Just as we were really beginning to experience a whole new dimension of life, you crash in here and destroy everything."

The hyena cups his paw to his ear, leans over closely to the lion, and shouts, "What say??"

On Verdi, Giuseppe, I'm keen:
  His name, if you know what I mean,
    Quite rolls off the tongue
    (It can almost be sung) —
  A pity it just means Joe Green.
      —Ron Rubin

A mother waited for hours outside the Philharmonic in hopes of meeting the conductor Zubin Mehta. Her patience was rewarded and she was finally able to corner Mehta for a moment.

"My son," she exclaims. "You have to hear him! He plays just like Itzhak Perlman."

"I'm sure he does," says Mehta, humoring her, "but if he wants to audition, there is a process. Just have him contact the Philharmonic office in the morning."

"I'll certainly do that, Maestro, but since we happen to be walking together..." —because by now she's following him down the street— "you might as well listen to this." And without waiting for an answer, she whips out an old cassette tape player and presses PLAY. "My son plays just like Perlman!"

Mehta listens for a bit and says, "Good Lord, that does sound like Perlman!"

"It is Perlman! My son plays just like that!"

What, and Quit Show Business?

A musician and a bunch of his buddies are jamming very loudly late one night when an angry man comes to their apartment door.

"Didn't you hear me pounding on the floor upstairs?" the man complains.

"Oh, that's okay," says the drummer, "we're making a lot of noise ourselves."

Even angrier, the man demands, "Do you know there's a little old lady sick upstairs?"

"No, man," says the pianist, "but hum a few bars and we'll fake it."

What's the difference between a rocker and a jazz musician?

—The rocker plays 3 chords in front of 3,000 people. The jazz musician plays 3,000 chords in front of three people.

"Extraordinary how potent cheap music is."
— Noel Coward

Why did the punk rocker cross the road?

—Because he was stapled to a chicken.

What do you call a drummer in a three-piece suit?

—The defendant.

MUSICIAN TIP: At the end of the night, your bar tab should be less than your pay.

"I don't like country music, but I don't like to denigrate those who do. And for the people who like country music, *denigrate* means *put down*."
—Bob Newhart

"I hate rap music, which to me sounds like a bunch of angry men shouting, possibly because the person who was supposed to provide them with a melody never showed up."
— Dave Barry`

NOTE TO SONGWRITERS: Every time you start a song with "Woke up this morning..." God kills a puppy.

Two songwriters watch a man fall off the roof of a ten-story building. The man crashes through the awning and hits the sidewalk, then brushes himself off and walks away.

"Wow, isn't he lucky?" says one songwriter.

"You call that lucky?" asks the other. "Andrew Lloyd Weber —now *he's* lucky."

off the mark.com   by Mark Parisi

Y'KNOW, IT'S REALLY KIND OF COSMIC HOW WE BOTH SEEM TO WAKE UP AT THE SAME TIME EVERY MORNING!

offthemark.com   ATLANTIC FEATURE © 1996 MARK PARISI

Mark Parisi

Write Your Own C&W Hit

by Larry Tritten

Your cheatin' heart got you down, Sue Ellen?
Just string the lyrics together and howl

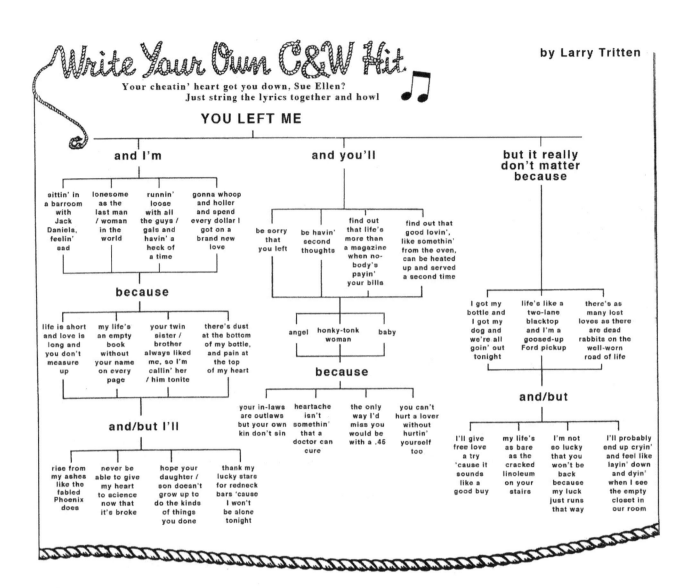

YOU LEFT ME

and I'm

- sittin' in a barroom with Jack Daniels, feelin' sad
- lonesome as the last man / woman in the world
- runnin' loose with all the guys / gals and havin' a heck of a time
- gonna whoop and holler and spend every dollar I got on a brand new love

because

- life is short and love is long and you don't measure up
- my life's an empty book without your name on every page
- your twin sister / brother always liked me, so I'm callin' her / him tonite
- there's dust at the bottom of my bottle, and pain at the top of my heart

and/but I'll

- rise from my ashes like the fabled Phoenix does
- never be able to give my heart to science now that it's broke
- hope your daughter / son doesn't grow up to do the kinds of things you done
- thank my lucky stars for redneck bars 'cause I won't be alone tonight

and you'll

- be sorry that you left
- be havin' second thoughts
- find out that life's more than a magazine when nobody's payin' your bills
- find out that good lovin', like somethin' from the oven, can be heated up and served a second time

angel / honky-tonk woman / baby

because

- your in-laws are outlaws but your own kin don't sin
- heartache isn't somethin' that a doctor can cure
- the only way I'd miss you would be with a .45
- you can't hurt a lover without hurtin' yourself too

but it really don't matter because

- I got my bottle and I got my dog and we're all goin' out tonight
- life's like a two-lane blacktop and I'm a goosed-up Ford pickup
- there's as many lost loves as there are dead rabbits on the well-worn road of life

and/but

- I'll give free love a try 'cause it sounds like a good buy
- my life's as bare as the cracked linoleum on your stairs
- I'm not so lucky that you won't be back because my luck just runs that way
- I'll probably end up cryin' and feel like layin' down and dyin' when I see the empty closet in our room

---

Why hat do you get when you play a country music song backwards?

You get your house back
You get your dog back
You get your best friend Jack back
You get your truck back
You get your hair back
Ya get your first and second wives back
Your front porch swing
Your pretty little thing
Your bling bling bling and a diamond ring
Your get your farm and the barn and the boat and the Harley
First night in jail with Charlie

You get your mind back
You get your nerves back
Your first heart attack back

You get your pride back
You get your life back
You get your first real love back
You get your big screen TV, a DVD and a washing machine
You get the pond and the lawn
And the bail and the mower
You go back where you don't know her

It sounds a little crazy a little scattered and absurd
But that's what you get
When you play a country song backwards.

—from *Backwards*, Rascal Flatts

What do you get when you play New Age music backwards?
—New Age music.

Damian Clark

What, and Quit Show Business?

"I'm going to begin with a joke
so we can get the humor out of the way."

Andrew Toos

A certain aspiring young comic, back in Depression days, found himself in a bad way. New bookings had vanished, his wife was pregnant, and his funds hovered perilously close to zero. Pocketing his pride, he made the rounds of the older and better established comedians whom he had come to know.

Bob Hope listened to his tale sympathetically and said, "Kid, things are a little tight with me, too, right now, and I can't help you just at present, but I'm amazed you're having trouble. I caught your act a couple of months ago and you're terrific. Once you get over this bad spot, you should have no trouble at all getting established."

George Burns was equally sympathetic. He said, "I wish I could help you, buddy, but I've had a streak of bad luck myself lately. But don't be discouraged. I've heard you deliver and I want to tell you that as far as I'm concerned, there's the making of a major talent in you. Keep it up, fella. "

Jack Benny listened and said, "Well, I'll write you out a check for what you need and if you need more, let me know. I've got to tell you, though, that I don't think you'll make it in this tough business of ours. You just don't have the spark."

Our young comic arrived home at last and said to his wife, "Well, I've got some money and it will see us through, maybe, till things turn better."

Then he added bitterly, "But once you're down, you sure find out quickly which so-called friends turn their back on you. That rotten, lousy Jack Benny…"

A man is auditioning his stage act with his "talking dog."

"What's on the top of a house?"

"Roof! Roof!"

"How do you describe sandpaper"

"Rough! Rough!"

"Who's the best baseball player ever?"

"Rufth! Rufth!"

The manager throws the man and his dog out onto the sidewalk.

The dog says, "Maybe I shoulda said DiMaggio?"

"Dying is easy; comedy is hard."
—last words of Edmund Kean

"Tragedy is when I cut my finger. Comedy is when you fall into an open sewer and die."
—Mel Brooks

They used to laugh when I said I wanted to be a comedian. Well, they're not laughing now!

106

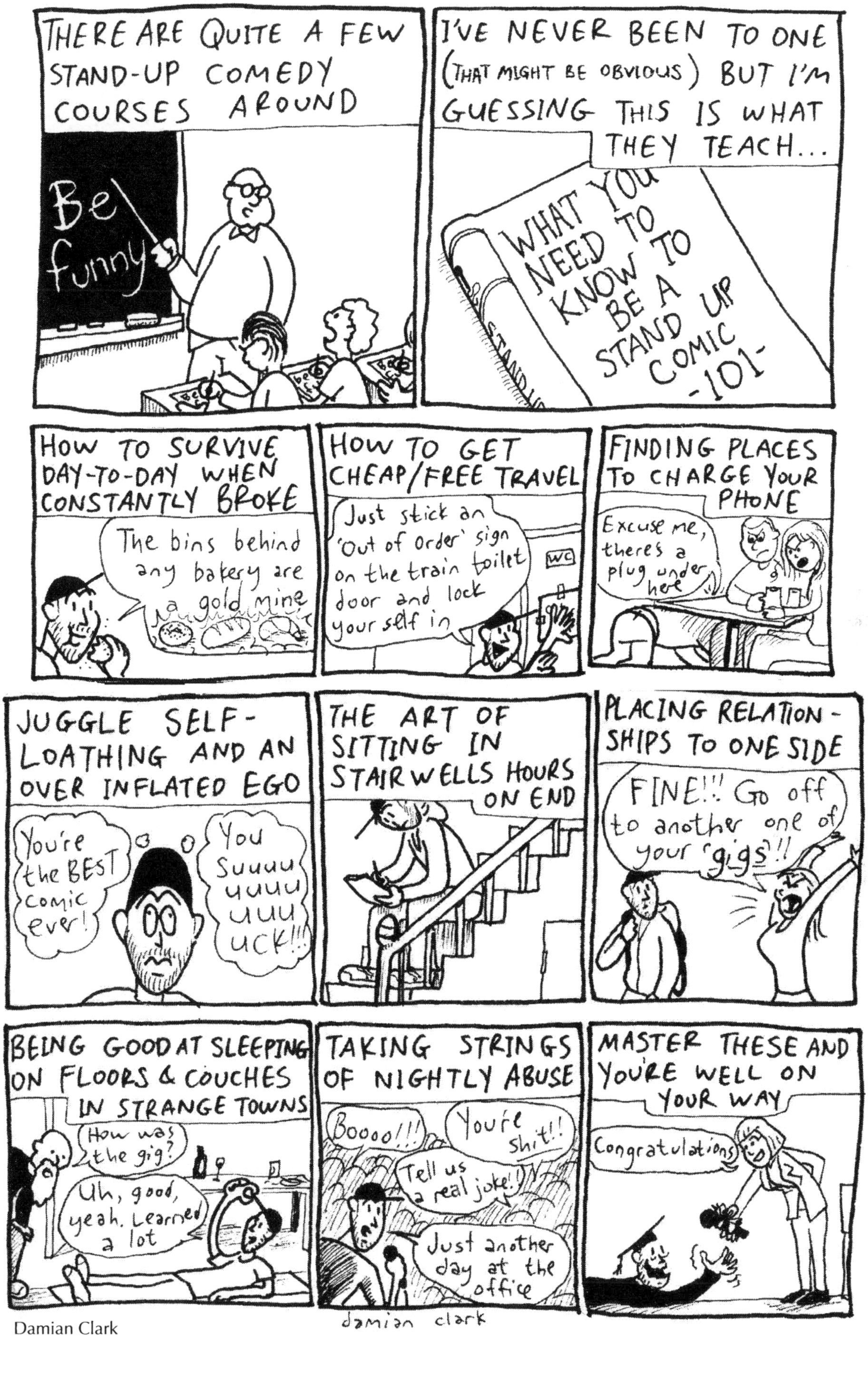
THERE ARE QUITE A FEW STAND-UP COMEDY COURSES AROUND
Be funny
I'VE NEVER BEEN TO ONE (THAT MIGHT BE OBVIOUS) BUT I'M GUESSING THIS IS WHAT THEY TEACH...
WHAT YOU NEED TO KNOW TO BE A STAND UP COMIC -101-
HOW TO SURVIVE DAY-TO-DAY WHEN CONSTANTLY BROKE
The bins behind any bakery are a gold mine
HOW TO GET CHEAP/FREE TRAVEL
Just stick an 'Out of Order' sign on the train toilet door and lock your self in
WC
FINDING PLACES TO CHARGE YOUR PHONE
Excuse me, there's a plug under here
JUGGLE SELF-LOATHING AND AN OVER INFLATED EGO
You're the BEST comic ever!
You Suuuuuuuuuuuck!!!
THE ART OF SITTING IN STAIRWELLS HOURS ON END
PLACING RELATIONSHIPS TO ONE SIDE
FINE!!! Go off to another one of your 'gigs'!!
BEING GOOD AT SLEEPING ON FLOORS & COUCHES IN STRANGE TOWNS
How was the gig?
Uh, good, yeah. Learned a lot
TAKING STRINGS OF NIGHTLY ABUSE
Boooo!!!
You're shit!!
Tell us a real joke!!
Just another day at the office
MASTER THESE AND YOU'RE WELL ON YOUR WAY
Congratulations
damian clark

Damian Clark

"If I have to explain the joke, it's not funny."

Bob Eckstein

A guy works in the circus, following the elephants with a pail and shovel. Year after year, same job. One day, his brother comes to see him, a big smile on his face.

"Sam, I've got great news," he announces. "I got you a plush job in my office. You'll get to wear nice clothes, work regular hours, and the money is great. No more sweat and toil, no more working outside in miserable weather, no more elephant dung. How about it?"

Sam looks at him in disbelief and says, "What? And quit show business?"

A man has just moved into the neighborhood and visits the local pub for the first time.

Soon he hears someone yell out "Number 23," for apparently no reason — but it's followed by a roar of laughter from around the room.

The newcomer asks one of the old-timers what's going on. "Well, it's like this: we've all been coming here for years, and we know each other's jokes. A while back we decided to put together a numbered list of our favorites, so that all you have to do is call out the number and everyone can remember it and have a good laugh."

"That's great!" says the newcomer. "Let me see the list and try one out." He looks at the list, chooses a favorite, and shouts out, "Number 11!"

There is a deathly silence, so he bravely tries again. "Number 11!" The silence continues.

"Why did they laugh at 23 and not at 11?" he asks the old-timer.

"Well, you see," explains the older man, "it isn't the joke so much as the way you tell it."

A man wrought with despair goes to the doctor. He tells the doctor how depressed he is, that life just seems cruel and pointless. He says he feels all alone in a threatening world where what lies ahead is uncertain or worse. He doesn't know if he can go on like this much longer.

The doctor examines him and finds nothing wrong. "You know, we all feel like that from time to time. We just need to get out of our skin and relax and laugh about it all. You're in luck, because the great clown Pagliacci is in town tonight. Go and see him perform. I promise that will pick up your spirits."

"But doctor," cries the man, "I am Pagliacci."

"What's the next best medicine?"

Charles Barsotti

108

"Now I'll never dance," said Tom defeatedly.

- "But I really really want to go to the dance!" Tom bawled.

- "I must admit I forgot the name of Fred Astaire's partner," Tom said gingerly.

- "I can't play the guitar because my fingers are too big," said Tom fretfully.

- "Elvis is dead," Tom said expressly.

- "Let's all play an A, a C#, and an E," cried the band in accord.

- "That may cause my violin strings to snap," was Tom's gut reaction.

- "May I join your singing group?" Tom inquired.

- "I have to sing a run of eighth-notes," said Tom quaveringly.

- "This movie will prove very popular," Tom projected.

- "This spring I'll be attending that French film festival," Tom added cannily.

- "Carnivals are noisy and useless," griped Tom unfairly.

- "I'm afraid this level of the theater is full," said the usher tearfully.

- "I no longer perform," said Tom exactingly.

- "I'm stuck here with my friend Hamlet," said Tom with disdain.

Liam Francis Walsh

How many screenwriters does it take to screw in a lightbulb?
—The bulb is IN and it's staying IN!

- How many art directors does it take to screw in a lightbulb?
—Does it have to be a lightbulb? I've got this neat candle holder...

- How many editors does it take to change a lightbulb?
—If we change the lightbulb, we'll have to change everything.

- How many over-eager PA's does it take to screw in a li...
—Done!

- How many entertainment lawyers does it take to screw in a lightbulb?
—How many can you afford?

- How many Shirley MacLaines does it take to screw in a lightbulb?
—Just the current one. The previous versions aren't all that familiar with electricity.

- How many musicians does it take to screw in a lightbulb?
—Fifteen. One to hold the bulb, four to turn the ladder and ten to be on the guest list.

- How many folk musicians does it take to change a lightbulb?
—Seven. One to change it and the other six to sing about how good the old one was.

- How many jugglers does it take to screw in a lightbulb?
—One, but it takes at least three lightbulbs.

- How many magicians does it take to change a lightbulb?
—Into what?

- How many actors does it take to screw in a lightbulb?
—Nine: one to screw it in and the other eight to hold the mirror.
— Only one. They don't like to share the spotlight.

- How many dancers does it take to screw in a lightbulb?
—Five!... Six!... Seven!... Eight!

Chapter Six

Brother, Can You Paradigm?

Words, Words, Words

"Could we please just decide on which word for
snow we're going to use and GO with that?"

Buddy Hickerson

Dan Piraro

When does a dialect become a language?

— When its speakers get an army and a navy.

"The Inuit have over 50 words for *visiting ethnolinguist.*"
— David Javerbaum

A woman walks into a cocktail bar and orders a Double Entendre. So the bartender gives it to her.

What do you get when you cross a joke with a rhetorical question?

DICTIONARY, n.   A malevolent literary device for cramping the growth of a language and making it hard and inelastic. This dictionary, however, is a most useful work.

— Ambrose Bierce, *The Devil's Dictionary*

Anatol Kovarsky

"*My God, do you suppose it can read?!*"

Archival material from Playboy magazine. Copyright © 1967
by Playboy. Reprinted with permission. All rights reserved.

Gahan Wilson

off the mark.com — by Mark Parisi

Mark Parisi

Sailor to his captain: "Here's a special message from the admiral, captain. It's to you personally, sir."

"Read it to me," snapped the captain.

The sailor read: "Of all the blundering, stupid, idiotic morons, you take the cake!"

"Have that decoded at once!" ordered the captain.

English is essentially German spoken in the mouth rather than the throat.

Swedish, Norwegian and Danish are actually the same language. It's just that the Norwegians can't spell it, and the Danes can't pronounce it.

Spanish is what happened when Moors tried to learn Latin and said "screw it."

Tagalog is essentially Visayan spoken by Kapampangans.

Czech is essentially Russian with beer instead of vodka.

Korean is essentially being caught in a syllable-diagramming exercise gone horribly, horribly wrong.

Franche est essentialement englaishe ouithe les endinges funnies et lottes de vowelles et les adjectifs en alle les places ronges.

Esperanto is essentially Indo-European pidgin.

Early one morning, the first mate notices the captain open the ship's safe, remove a small piece of paper, carefully read it, put it back in the safe, lock the safe, and then proceed to the bridge to assume his duties.

A few mornings later, he happens to spy the captain doing the same thing all over again. Curious, he starts to keep an eye on the captain and, sure enough, discovers that the exact same ritual is repeated each and every morning. Determined to get to the bottom of the mystery, he continues his spying and one day is able to figure out the combination to the safe.

That night, with the captain soundly sleeping, he quietly opens the safe and removes the piece of paper.

On it he reads: "Port left, starboard right."

"Life is too short to learn German."
—Oscar Wilde

114   *Brother, Can You Paradigm?*

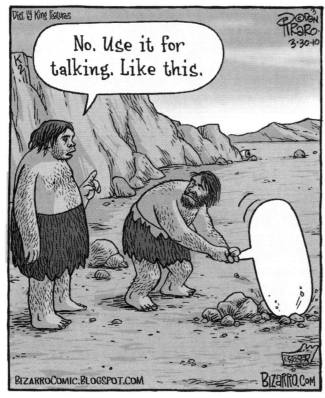

> No. Use it for talking. Like this.

Dist. by King Features

BIZARROCOMIC.BLOGSPOT.COM

BIZARRO.COM

Dan Piraro

A Spanish-speaking bandit held up a bank in El Paso. The sheriff and his deputy eventually tracked him down. When they captured him, the sheriff, who couldn't speak Spanish, had his bi-lingual deputy ask the bandit where he'd hidden the money.

"No sé nada," the bandit defiantly replied.

The sheriff put a gun to the bandit's head and said to his deputy: "Tell him that if he doesn't tell us where the money is right now, I'll blow his brains out."

Upon receiving the translation into Spanish, the bandit was shaking in his boots and cried out. "¡Ya me acuerdo. Tienen que caminar tres cuadras hasta ese gran arbol: allí está el dinero!"

The sheriff leaned forward. "Yeah? Well..?"

The deputy replied: "He says he wants to die like a man."

Two highway workers are busy working at a construction site when a limo with diplomatic license plates pulls up.

"Parlez-vous français?" the driver asks them. The two workers just stare.

"Sprechen sie deutsch?" The two continue to stare at him.

"Fala português?" Neither worker says anything.

"Parlate italiano?" Still no response.

Finally, the man drives off in disgust. One worker turns to the other and says, "Gee, maybe we should learn a foreign language..."

"What for? That guy knew four of 'em and what good did it do him?"

A mouse is in his mouse hole and he wants to go out to get something to eat, but he's afraid there might be a cat lurking outside. He puts his ear by the opening and all he hears is "Bow Wow," so he thinks, "Well, there wouldn't be a cat out there because there's a big, bad dog."

He goes out of his mouse hole and is promptly caught and eaten by a cat, who licks his lips and says "It pays to be bi-lingual!!

Is French kissing in France just called kissing?

What if soy milk is just regular milk introducing itself in Spanish?

THE HYPNOTIST

BOCK BOCK BOCK!

BOCK BOCK BOCK!

WHAT A HOAX! HE'S SPEAKING TOTAL GIBBERISH.

Hilary Price

Two elderly Jewish men are sitting in an old-world Jewish deli, chatting away in Yiddish. A Chinese waiter comes over and greets them in fluent Yiddish.

The Jewish men are dumbfounded. They are both thinking the same thing: "My God, where did he learn such perfect Yiddish?" They have their meal and the Chinese waiter's Yiddish continues to be as impeccable as his service. When they pay the bill, the manager asks them if everything was to their satisfaction. The men praise the food and service, but can't resist asking, "Where did our waiter learn such fabulous Yiddish?"

The owner looks around, leans in so no one else will hear, and says, "Shhhh! He thinks we're teaching him English."

A Roman walks into a bar and asks for a martinus. "You mean a martini?" asks the bartender. The Roman replies, "If I wanted a double, I would have asked for it."

A husband and wife sign up for Chinese language lessons. "Are you planning to go to China?" the instructor asks.

"Oh, no." says the man. "We just adopted a baby from China and when she starts talking we want to be able to understand what she's saying."

An American diplomat tells a joke in a public meeting in an African state. He takes his time and tells the joke very slowly and at great length. Eventually he finishes and the interpreter translates in a few words and a roar of laughter breaks out.

"How did you manage to tell the joke so briefly?" asks the diplomat.

"Oh," says the interpreter, "I just said, `He told a joke. Laugh!'"

off the mark .com   by Mark Parisi
offthemark.com

SON, I'D LIKE YOU TO MEET THE FRENCH AMBASSADOR...

@#$!

AIDEN'S DAD QUICKLY REGRETTED ALL THE TIMES HE SAID "PARDON MY FRENCH"

Mark Parisi

116   Brother, Can You Paradigm?

Four linguists were sharing a compartment on a train on their way to an international conference. One was English, one Spanish, one French and the fourth German. They got into a discussion on whose language was the most eloquent and euphonious.

The English linguist said: "English is the most eloquent language. Take for instance the word *butterfly*. *Butterfly, butterfly*... doesn't that word so beautifully express the way this delicate insect flies. It's like *flutter-by, flutter-by*."

"Oh, no!" said the Spanish linguist, "the word for *butterfly* in Spanish is *mariposa*. Can't you hear how beautifully this word reflects the vibrant colors on the butterfly's wings? What could be a more apt name for such a brilliant creature? Spanish is the most eloquent language!"

"*Papillon*!" says the French linguist, "*Papillon* expresses the fragility of the butterfly's wings and body. This is the most fitting name for such a delicate and ethereal insect. French is the most eloquent of languages!"

At this the German llinguist stands up and demands: "Und vot is rongk mit SCHMETTERLING?"

A chieftain from an isolated South Pacific island nation flew to the United States on a diplomatic mission. When he arrived at the airport in Washington D.C., a host of newsmen and television cameramen met him. One of the reporters asked the chieftain if he had enjoyed a comfortable flight. The chieftain made a series of weird noises: "screech, scratch, honk, buzz, whistle, z-z-z-z..." and then added, "Yes, the flight was quite comfortable, the crew very accommodating, and the meal very tasty."

Another reporter asked, "What sites do you most want to visit during your stay here?" The chieftain made the same noises: "screech, scratch, honk, buzz, whistle, z-z-z-z..." and then said, "I would very much like to tour the White House, and peruse as much of the Smithsonian collection as time allows."

"Where did you learn to speak such flawless English?" asked the next reporter.

The chieftain replied, "Screech, scratch, honk, buzz, whistle, z-z-z-z...from the short-wave radio."

Mr. Goldberg, from Odessa, coming to America, shared a table in the ship's dining room with a Frenchman. Mr. Goldberg could speak neither French nor English; the Frenchman could speak neither Russian nor Yiddish.

The first day out, the Frenchman approached the table, bowed and said, "Bon appétit!"

Goldberg, puzzled for a moment, bowed back and replied "Goldberg." Every day, at every meal, the same routine occurred.

On the fifth day, a Russian-speaking passenger took Goldberg aside. "Listen, the Frenchman isn't telling you his name. He's saying 'Good Appetite,' He's saying, "Enjoy your meal."

At the next meal, Mr. Goldberg, beaming, bowed to the Frenchman and said, "Bon appétit!".

And the Frenchman, beaming, replied: "Goldberg!"

Dan Piraro

"What I don't, like, get is how she, like, figured out I was, like, having an affair with, like, the babysitter."

Danny Shanahan

Hypothetical Chinese

I thought you were on a diet.
—Wai Yu Mun Ching?

Are you harboring a fugitive?
—Hu Yu Hai Ding?

Your price is too high!!!
—No Bai Dam Ting!!!

Do you know the lyrics to the Macarena?
—Wai Yu Sing Dum Song?

See me A.S.A.P.
—Kum Hia Nao.

Did you go to the beach?
—Wai Yu So Tan?

I got this for free.
—Ai No Pei.

Please stay a little longer.
—Wai Go Nao?

I am not guilty.
—Wai Hang Mi?

Dan Piraro

Brother, Can You Paradigm?

LOST IN TRANSLATION

DRY CLEANER'S, BANGKOK:
Drop your trousers here for the best results.

HOTEL ROOM NOTICE, THAILAND:
We will execute your solicitors with pleasure.

DETOUR SIGN IN KYUSHI, JAPAN:
Stop. Drive sideways.

HOTEL, JAPAN:
You are invited to take advantage of the chambermaids. They are here to service you.

AMERICAN ADVERTISING IN FOREIGN COUNTRIES:

• The American Dairy Association was so successful with its "Got Milk?" campaign, that it was decided to extend the ads to Mexico. Unfortunately, the Spanish translation was "Are you lactating?"

• Coors put its slogan, "Turn it loose," into Spanish, where it was read as "Suffer from diarrhea."

• Frank Perdue's line, "It takes a tough man to make a tender chicken" in Spanish became "It takes a sexually stimulated man to make a chicken affectionate."

During World War I, a German soldier on the eastern front expressed his absolute certainty of victory. "Franz," he said, "we Germans are pious people who pray to God on the eve of each battle. How can we lose?"

Franz said, "I know that, Dietrich, but the Russians are pious, too. They also pray to God before each battle."

Dietrich said, "Of course, Franz, but who understands Russian?"

The expression "out of sight, out of mind" was fed into an English-to-Chinese translation app and then reverse translated from Chinese back to English.
The result: "Blind idiot."

Don't mess with me! I know judo, karate, aikido, kendo and six other words in Japanese.

Kirk Anderson

119

Dan Piraro

A doting husband buys an extraordinary talking bird for his wife's birthday. It speaks seven languages and costs him several thousand dollars.

"Did you get the bird I sent you?" he excitedly asks her that evening.

"Yes," says his wife enthusiastically. "Thanks so much, darling. I already have it in the oven."

"What?! Oh my God, that bird could speak seven languages!"

"Then why didn't it say something?"

The first rule of Thesaurus Club is: You don't talk about, mention, speak of, discuss, chin-wag, natter, or chat about Thesaurus Club.

CHICKEN 1: Buk

CHICKEN 2: Buk

CHICKEN 1: Buk Buk

CHICKEN 2: Why are you changing the subject?

What does DNA stand for?
—National Dyslexia Association.

INTERVIEWER: The spelling in your application is very erratic. Are you sure you don't have dyslexia?

APPLICANT: Have it? I can't even smell it!

I have sexdaily. I mean, dyslexia. Fcuk!

What do we want?
—A cure for Tourette's!

When do we want it?
—Cunt!

"Shut up, he explained."
—Ring Lardner

"Fuck you, she explained."
—Mrs. McEvoy

What honeymoon advice did the gruff editor Pete give to his young proofreader, the very shy Larry?
—"STET!"

THE Komma Sutra

English is a Stupid Language

Let's face it

English is a stupid language.

There is no egg in the eggplant

No ham in the hamburger

And neither pine nor apple in the pineapple.

English muffins were not invented in England

French fries were not invented in France.

We sometimes take English for granted

But if we examine its paradoxes we find that

Quicksand takes you down slowly

Boxing rings are square

And a guinea pig is neither from Guinea nor is it a pig.

Sweetmeats are candies, while sweetbreads,

Which aren't sweet, are meat.

If a vegetarian eats vegetables

What the heck does a humanitarian eat!?

Why do people recite at a play

Yet play at a recital?

Park on driveways and drive on parkways?

How can the weather be as hot as hell on one day,

And as cold as hell on another?

You have to marvel at the unique lunacy

Of a language where a house can burn up as it burns down

And in which you fill in a form

By filling it out

And a bell is only heard once it goes off!

How can a slim chance and a fat chance be the same,

While a wise man and a wise guy are opposites?

English was invented by people, not computers,

off the mark .com   by Mark Parisi

ALERT: YOU HAVE JUST MISPRONOUNCED A WORD IN YOUR HEAD. WOULD YOU LIKE THE CORRECT PRONUNCIATION?

MarkParisi@aol.com
©2005 MARK PARISI DIST. BY UFS INC.   offthemark.com

BOOKS WE CAN LOOK FORWARD TO

Mark Parisi

And it reflects the creativity of the human race

(Which of course isn't a race at all)

That is why

When the stars are out they are visible

But when the lights are out they are invisible

And why it is that when I wind up my watch

It starts

But when I wind up this poem

It ends.

The great writer Samuel Johnson was once taking a carriage ride from London to Bristol when a lady sitting across from him could not help but comment, "Sir, you smell!"

"Madam," he corrected her, "I stink. You smell."

I shot the serif.

ODE TO THE SPELL CHECK

Eye halve a spelling chequer
It cam with my pea sea
It plainly marques four my revue
Miss steaks eye kin knot sea.
Eye strike a key and type a word
And weight four it two say
Weather eye am wrong oar write
It shows me strait a weigh.
As soon as a mist ache is maid
It nose bee fore two long
And eye can put the error rite
Its rare lea ever wrong.
Eye have run this poem threw it
I am shore your pleased two no
Its letter perfect awl the weigh
My chequer tolled me sew!

Dear John,
   I want a man who knows what love is all about. You are generous, kind, thoughtful. People who are not like you admit to being useless and inferior.

You have ruined me for other men. I yearn for you. I have no feelings whatsoever when we're apart. I can be forever happy —will you let me be yours?

Gloria

Dear John,
   I want a man who knows what love is. All about you are generous, kind, thoughtful people, who are not like you. Admit to being useless and inferior.

You have ruined me. For other men, I yearn. For you, I have no feelings whatsoever. When we're apart, I can be forever happy. Will you let me be?

Yours,
Gloria

"I don't give a damn for a man that can only spell a word one way."
   — Mark Twain

Mark Parisi

Brother, Can You Paradigm?

Grammar Pirate

Scott Clark

The European Commission has just announced an agreement whereby English will be the official language of the European Union rather than German, which was the other possibility. As part of the negotiations, Her Majesty's Government conceded that English spelling had some room for improvement and has accepted a 5-year phase-in plan that would be known as "Euro-English."

In the first year, "s" will replace the soft "c." Sertainly this will make the sivil servants jump with joy. The hard "c" will be dropped in favor of the "k". This should klear up konfusion and keyboards kan have one less letter.

There will be growing publik enthusiasm in the sekond year when the troublesome "ph" will be replased with "f". This will make words like "fotograf" 20% shorter!

In the 3rd year, publik akseptanse of the new spelling kan be expected to reach the stage where more komplikated changes are possible. Governments will enkourage the removal of double leters which have always ben a deterent to akurate speling. Also, all wil agre that the horible mes of the silent "e" in the language is disgrasful and it should be dropd.

By the 4th year, the people will be reseptiv to steps such as replasing "th" with "z" and "w" wiz "v". During ze fifz year ze unesesary "o" kan be dropd from vords containing "ou", and similar changes vud of kurs be aplid to ozer kombinations of leters. After ze fifz yer ve vil hav a rali sensibl ritn styl. Zer vil be no mor trubl or difikultis and evriun vil find it ezi tu undrstand ech ozer.

Zen Z Drem Vil Finali Kum Tru!!

the ONION

Clinton Deploys Vowels to Bosnia

Cities of Sjlbvdnzv, Grznc to Be First Recipients

WASHINGTON, D.C.
DECEMBER 5, 1995

Before an emergency joint session of Congress yesterday, President Clinton announced U.S. plans to deploy more than 75,000 vowels to the war-torn region of Bosnia. The deployment, the largest of its kind in American history, will provide the region with the critically needed letters A, E, I, O and U, and is hoped to render countless Bosnian names more pronounceable.

"For six years, we have stood by while names like Ygrjvslhv, Tzlynhr and Glrm have been horribly butchered by millions around the world," Clinton said. "Today, the United States must finally stand up and say, 'Enough.' It is time the people of Bosnia finally had some vowels in their incomprehensible words. The US is proud to lead the crusade in this noble endeavor."

The deployment, dubbed Operation Vowel Storm by the State Department, is set for early next week, with the Adriatic port cities of Sjlbvdnzv and Grznc slated to be the first recipients. Two C-130 transport planes, each carrying more than 500 24-count boxes of E's, will fly from Andrews Air Force Base across the Atlantic and airdrop the letters over the cities.

Citizens of Grznc and Sjlbvdnzv eagerly await the arrival of the vowels. "My God, I do not think we can last another day," Trszg Grzdnjlkn, 44, said. "I have six children and none of them has a name that is understandable to me or anyone else. Mr. Clinton, please send my poor, wretched family just one E. Please."

Said Sjlbvdnzv resident Grg Hmphrs, 67: "With just a few key letters, I could

be George Humphries. This is my dream."

If the initial airlift is successful, Clinton said the U.S. will go ahead with full-scale vowel deployment, with C-130s airdropping thousands more letters over every area of Bosnia. Other nations are expected to pitch in, as well, including 10,000 British A's and 6,500 Canadian U's. Japan, rich in A's and O's, was asked to participate in the relief effort but declined.

"With these valuable letters, the people of war-ravaged Bosnia will be able to make some terrific new words," Clinton said. "It should be very exciting for them and surely much easier for us to read their maps."

Linguists praise the U.S.'s decision to send the vowels. "Vowels are crucial to the construction of all language," Baylor University linguist Noam Frankel said. "Please, don't get me started on the moon-man language they use in those Eastern European countries."

According to Frankel, once the Bosnians have vowels, they will be able to construct such valuable sentences as "The potatoes are ready," "I believe it will rain," and "All my children are dead from the war."

The American airdrop represents the largest deployment of any letter to a foreign country since 1984. During the summer of that year, the U.S. shipped 92,000 consonants to Ethiopia, providing cities like Ouaououaua, Eaoiiuae, and Aao with vital, life-giving supplies of L's, S's and T's. The consonant-relief effort failed, however, when vast quantitites of the letters were intercepted and hoarded by gun-toting warlords.

Text reprinted with permission of The Onion.
© 2015 by Onion, Inc. www.theonion.com

"The only man, woman, or child who ever wrote a simple declarative sentence with seven grammatical errors is dead."

— e. e. cummings on the death of U.S. President Warren G. Harding in 1923

Critic to Winston Churchill: "Never end a sentence with a preposition."

Winston Churchill to critic: "This is the kind of arrant pedantry up with which I will not put."

Sam was having the kind of problems Viagra was meant to solve, but this was in the pre-Viagra era, so he had to search high and low for a remedy. His quest eventually led him to a Seminole shaman who promised him a "partial cure."

Sam naturally asks, "What do you mean by partial?"

"This is strong stuff. It absolutely works, but you can only use it once a year," explains the shaman. "All you have to do is say '1-2-3' and it shall rise in all its glory for as long as you wish!"

Sam figures once a year is better than nothing. "That's great!" he exclaims, but then thinks to ask, "What happens when I'm done?"

The medicine man replies: "All you or your partner has to say is '1-2-3-4' and it will go down. But remember —it will not work again for another year!"

Sam rushes home, eager to enjoy his recaptured potency. He hops into bed with his wife, and lying next to her he says, "1-2-3."

He immediately becomes more robustly aroused than at any time in his life, just as the shaman had promised. Sam's wife, who had been facing away, turns over and asks, "What did you say '1-2-3' for?"

And now you know why you should never end a sentence with a preposition.

A Texan was visiting Harvard University, and was lost. He stopped a student and asked, "Do you know where the library is at?"

"I sure do," replied the student, "But, you know, you're not supposed to end sentences with prepositions."

"What?"

"Prepositions. You ended your sentence with *at*, which is a preposition, and you're not supposed to do that."

"Oh, okay," said the Texan. "In that case, do you know where the library is at, asshole?"

"If a word in the dictionary were misspelled, how would we know?"
—Steven Wright

The Titel of this Section Contains Three Erors.

off the mark .com   by Mark Parisi

ZZXVZJQ! AND A TRIPLE WORD SCORE, TOO!

THE WORST PART OF BEING ABDUCTED BY ALIENS

Mark Parisi

125

CALLAHAN

"NOW, CLASS, IS THIS MAN LYING OR LAYING IN THE GUTTER?"

John Callahan

FROM THE LYRICS TO COMDEN & GREEN'S *One Hundred Easy Ways To Lose A Man:*

You've found your perfect mate and it's been love from the start.

He whispers, "You're the one to who I give my heart."

Don't say, "I love you too, my dear, let's never, never part."

Just say, "I'm afraid you've made a grammatical error. It's not to *who* I give my heart, it's to *whom* I give my heart. You see, with the use of the preposition *to*, *who* becomes the indirect object, making the use of the word *whom* imperative, which I can easily show you by drawing a very simple chart."

That's a fine way to lose a man...

Just show him where his grammar errs,
Then mark your towels *hers* and *hers*.

"As far as I'm concerned, *whom* is a word that was invented to make everyone sound like a butler."
—Calvin Trillin

Knock, knock.
　　Who's there?
　　To.
　　To who?
　　To whom.

Is there another word for *synonym*?

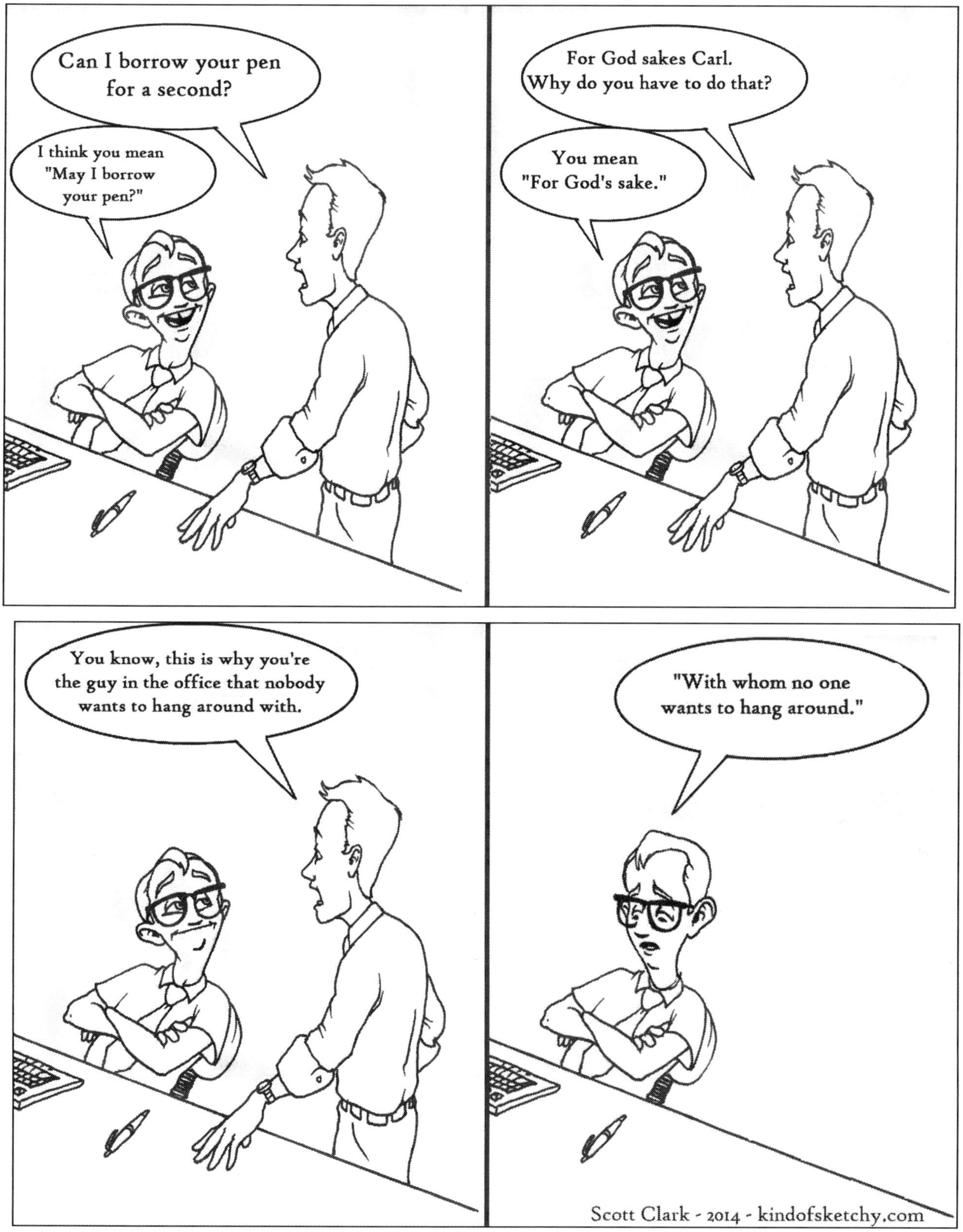
Can I borrow your pen for a second?
I think you mean "May I borrow your pen?"
For God sakes Carl. Why do you have to do that?
You mean "For God's sake."
You know, this is why you're the guy in the office that nobody wants to hang around with.
"With whom no one wants to hang around."
Scott Clark - 2014 - kindofsketchy.com

Scott Clark

Cyanide and Happiness © Explosm.net

Cyanide & Happiness

Let's eat grandma!
  Let's eat, grandma!
    Punctuation saves lives.

Punctuate the following sentence so that it makes sense:

James while John had had had had had had had had had had the teacher's approval.

ANSWER:

James, while John had had "had," had had "had had"; "had had" had had the teacher's approval.

The village blacksmith finally found an apprentice willing to work hard for long hours. The blacksmith immediately began his instructions to the lad, "When I take the shoe out of the fire, I'll lay it on the anvil; and when I nod my head, you hit it with this hammer."

The apprentice did just as he was told. Now he's the village blacksmith.

The other day my friend was telling me that I didn't understand what irony meant.

Which is ironic, because we were standing at a bus stop.

Paul Soderblom

Dear People of the World,
I don't mean to sound slutty, but please use me whenever you want.
Sincerely,
Grammar

Grammar: The difference between
...knowing you're shit and knowing your shit.
...having extra marital sex and having extra-marital sex.

I would rather cuddle then have sex. If you're good with grammar, you'll get it.

There was this guy from the midwest who had never eaten fresh fish straight from the ocean. He flies into Logan Airport in Boston, gets in a cab, and says: "I'm new in town and I'd like to get scrod."

The taxi driver looks at him blankly.

The midwestern guy says, "Don't you know what I'm talking about?"

The driver says, "Sure I do, I just never heard it in the pluperfect subjunctive before."

A teacher writes on a chalkboard the sentence: "A woman without her man is nothing" and asks the students to punctuate it.

The men write: "A woman, without her man, is nothing"

The women write: "A woman: without her, man is nothing."

LINGUISTICS TEACHER:
The double negative construction in some languages has a positive meaning and in others a very negative meaning. However, in no language is it the case that a double positive construction has a negative meaning.

VOICE FROM THE BACK OF THE CLASS: Yeah, yeah.

"Only kings, presidents, editors, and people with tapeworms have the right to use the editorial *we*."
—Mark Twain

Hospitals: the only place where the word "positive" means a bad thing.

NOTHING BOTHERED ARNOLD MORE THAN A MISPLACED COMMA.

Hilary Price

Tune in tonight at 8 for the premiere of "The Palindrome Family," featuring Mom, Pop, Anna, Bob, Eve, and their dog, Otto, as they pop Xanax and take kayak trips.

Huh?

Aha.

Dan Piraro

I just got my Ph.D. in palindromes. I'm now addressed as Dr. Awkward.

A verb enters a bar and spots a noun just sitting there, not doing anything. The verb goes over to the noun and smiles. "Hey," it says to the noun, "wanna come back to my place and conjugate?" The noun says "Sorry, but I'll have to decline."

Werner Heisenberg, Kurt Gödel, and Noam Chomsky walk into a bar. Heisenberg turns to the other two and says, "Clearly this is a joke, but how can we figure out whether or not it's funny?"

Gödel replies, "We can't know that because we're inside the joke."

Chomsky says, "Of course it's funny. You're just telling it wrong."

Two women walk into a bar and talk about the Bechdel test.

What's the difference between an etymologist and an entomologist?
— The etymologist knows the difference.

What do you call two crows on a branch?
— Attempted murder.

WITH THE OXFORD COMMA: "We invited the strippers, JFK, and Stalin."
WITHOUT THE OXFORD COMMA: "We invited the strippers, JFK and Stalin."

What do you say when comforting a Grammar Nazi?
— Their, there, they're.

How do you tell the difference between a plumber and a chemist?
—Ask them to pronounce *unionized*.

Yes, English pronunciation can be weird. It can be understood through tough thorough thought, though.

Five scholars, on a walk off campus, encountered a group of ladies clearly of that class described as being of easy virtue.

"Ah," said one of the scholars, "a jam of tarts."

"Not at all," said the second, "say, rather, a flourish of strumpets."

"Or," said the third, "an essay of Trollope's."

And the fourth said, "Rather, I think, an anthology of prose."

The fifth: "Clearly it's a frost of hoars."

If lawyers are disbarred and clergymen defrocked, doesn't it follow that electricians can be delighted; musicians denoted; cowboys deranged; models deposed; tree surgeons debarked and dry cleaners depressed? Laundry workers could decrease, eventually becoming depleted! Even more, bedmakers will be debunked, baseball players will be debased, landscapers will be deflowered, software engineers will be detested, and even musical composers will eventually decompose.

"If I had more time, I would have written a shorter letter."

— Cato, Cicero, Pliny the Younger, Blaise Pascal, Voltaire, Benjamin Franklin, Mark Twain, Johann Wolfgang von Goethe, George Bernard Shaw, Winston Churchill, Bill Clinton, etc.

An English professor complained to the pet shop proprietor, "The parrot I purchased uses improper language."

"That's hard to believe," said the owner. "I've certainly never taught that bird to swear."

"Oh, it isn't that," explained the professor. "But yesterday I heard him split an infinitive."

"Why is the alphabet in that order? Is it because of that song? The guy who wrote that song wrote everything."
—Steven Wright

"It's not the most intellectual job in the world, but I do have to know the letters."
—Vanna White (*Wheel of Fortune*)

So a dyslexic man walks into a bra...

Dyslexics Of The World, Untie!

Ambiguity: What happens in Vagueness stays in Vagueness.

"I before *e* except after *c* —that's weird," said the sheik.

The past, the present, and the future walked into a bar. It was tense.

"I used to be a proofreader for a skywriting company."
—Steven Wright

My English teacher looked my way and said, "Name two pronouns."
I said, "Who, me?"

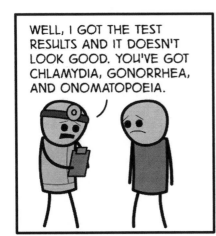
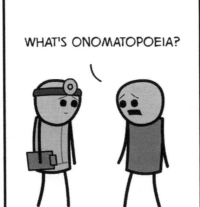

Cyanide & Happiness

It's hard to explain puns to kleptomaniacs because they always take things literally.

What's the difference between a cat and a comma?
—One has claws at the end of its paws, and the other is a pause at the end of a clause.

Three little kittens go boating on the Seine. There's an American cat named "one two three," a German cat named "ein zwei drei," and a French cat named "un deux trois." The boat tips over and all three cats have to swim for their lives. The American cat makes it to the Rive Gauche and the German cat to the Rive Droit, but the French cat is nowhere to be found.

Why?

Because the un deux trois quatre cinq.

Why is *abbreviated* such a long word?

Why does *monosyllabic* have five syllables?

Why is *brassiere* singular and *panties* plural?

Why isn't *phonetic* spelled the way it sounds?

Why are they called *apartments*, when they're all stuck together?

Why do they call it a *building*? It looks like they're finished. Why isn't it a *built*?

Why is it when you transport something by car, it's called a *shipment*, but when you transport something by ship, it's called *cargo*?

If *price* and *worth* mean the same thing, why are *priceless* and *worthless* opposites?

"I'm not afraid to use a different font," said Tom boldly.

• "This, that, these, those, and such," said Tom demonstratively.

• "I've never been good at crossword puzzles" said Tom cluelessly.

• "The way cartoonists censor their profanity is so @#$%&!" swore Tom comically.

• "One can't dispute the fundamental importance of learning the alphabet," Abie ceded.

• "Every syllable has at least one vowel," said Tom in rhythm.

• "I think we've broken the code," Tom said enigmatically.

• "Dot-dot-dot, dash-dash-dash, dot-dash-dot, dot-dash-dot, dash-dot-dash-dash," said Tom with remorse.

• "There's gotta be a word in English that uses all the vowels, including Y," announced Tom unquestionably. "But there's no word that has them all in the right order," he added facetiously.

How many Chomsky linguists does it take to change a lightbulb?
— One to buy the bulb and the rest follows from general principles.

• How many translators does it take to change a lightbulb?
—It depends upon the context.
—Is the lightbulb in editable format?

• How many proofreaders does it take to change a lightbulb?
—Proofreaders aren't supposed to change lightbulbs. They should just query them.

• How many English teachers does it take to change a lightbulb?
—Too.

Chapter Seven

An Infinite Number of Writers

Literature & the Literati

Dan Piraro

THE COMEBACK

WHAT WE SAY:
"If you give an infinite number of monkeys an infinite amount of typewriters for an infinite amount of time, they could create the complete works of Shakespeare."

Dist. by King Features
2.24.2014
©HILARY B. PRICE
rhymeswithorange.com

WHAT THE MONKEYS SAY:
"An infinite amount of monkeys over an infinite amount of time created Shakespeare himself, via evolution. So, duh, we've done it already."

Hilary Price

BREAKING NEWS: Archaeologists digging at the site of Shakespeare's house have uncovered the skeletons of thousands of monkeys.

From *Wikipedia*: In 2003, lecturers and students from the University of Plymouth MediaLab Arts course used a £2,000 grant from the Arts Council to study the literary output of real monkeys. They left a computer keyboard in the enclosure of six Celebes Crested Macaques in Paignton Zoo for a month.

Not only did the monkeys produce nothing but five total pages, largely consisting of the letter "S", but the lead male began by bashing the keyboard with a stone, and the monkeys continued by urinating and defecating on it. Mike Phillips, director of the university's Institute of Digital Arts and Technology, said that the artist-funded project was primarily performance art, and they had learned "an awful lot" from it. He concluded that monkeys "are not random generators. They're more complex than that. They were quite interested in the screen, and they saw that when they typed a letter, something happened. There was a level of intention."

"The profession of book writing makes horse racing seem like a solid, stable business."
—John Steinbeck

A writer dies and Saint Peter offers him the choice of Heaven or Hell. To see what he has in store, Saint Peter first takes him to Hell, where rows of writers are chained to their desks being whipped by demons in a steaming dungeon. However, when they get to Heaven the writer is astonished to see that nothing has changed —rows of writers are chained to their desks in a steaming dungeon being whipped.

"Hey!" says the writer, "this is just as bad as Hell!"

"No, it's not," replies Saint Peter. "Up here you get published."

What's the difference between publishers and terrorists?
—You can negotiate with terrorists.

"Are there any other Tales I wish I'd included...? Ooh, great question!"

Rob Murray

136

SCENES FROM A LITERARY BAR

CHARLES DICKENS: Please, sir, I'd like a martini.

BARTENDER: Sure thing. Olive or twist?

———————

JAMES JOYCE: I'll take a Guinness.

BARTENDER: So Charles Dickens was in here yesterday.

JAMES JOYCE: (drinks)

BARTENDER: And he asked for a martini and I said, "Olive or twist?"

JAMES JOYCE: (drinks)

BARTENDER: You see, it's funny because he wrote a book called "Oliver Twist."

JAMES JOYCE: What a shitty joke.

———————

ERNEST HEMINGWAY: Mojito.

BARTENDER: So Charles Dickens was in here two days ago.

ERNEST HEMINGWAY: Joyce already told me that joke. Fuck off.

———————

MARK TWAIN: Give me a brandy.

BARTENDER: So Charles Dickens came in the other day and ordered a martini.

MARK TWAIN: Did he take an olive or twist? Ha ha ha!

BARTENDER: (tearful) You did that on purpose, didn't you?

———————

VIRGINIA WOOLF: I'll take your second-best cognac and some unadulterated experience.

BARTENDER: We don't have that. This is a bar.

VIRGINIA WOOLF: Patriarchy! (drowns herself)

According to Hemingway, why did the chicken cross the road?

—To die, alone, in the rain.

INTERVIEWER: Why don't you write like you talk?

GERTRUDE STEIN: Why don't you read like I write?

"For most of history, *Anonymous* was a woman."

—Virginia Woolf

"The difference between literature and journalism is that journalism is unreadable and literature is not read."

—Oscar Wilde

Actually, the Civil War was a draw. The North won it in the history books but the South won it in the novels.

Doug Savage

Charles Addams

An Infinite Number of Writers

WILDE

If Oscar was wild,
was Thornton Wilder?
If Oscar was witty,
was John Greenleaf Whittier?
If Oscar was male,
is Norman Mailer?

—Michael Braude

If, with the literate, I am
Impelled to try an epigram,
I never seek to take the credit;
We all assume that Oscar said it.

—Dorothy Parker

Few understand the works of Cummings,
And few James Joyce's mental
slummings,
And few young Auden's coded chatter;
But then it is the few that matter.

—Dylan Thomas

"Biography lends to death a new terror."
—Oscar Wilde

ALEX: You were squealing, you were
screaming —admit it!
NAN: I was in seventh grade! And *Lady
Chatterly* isn't porn! It's literature!
MUMBLE: Only if you finish it.

—Paul Rudnick, *The Naked Eye*

"Although written many years ago,
Lady Chatterley's Lover has just been
reissued by the Grove Press, and this pictorial
account of the day-to-day life of an English
gamekeeper is full of considerable interest
to outdoor-minded readers, as it contains
many passages on pheasant-raising, the
apprehending of poachers, ways to control
vermin, and other chores and duties of the
professional gamekeeper. Unfortunately, one
is obliged to wade through many pages of
extraneous material in order to discover and
savour those sidelights on the management
of a midland shooting estate, and in
this reviewer's opinion the book cannot
take the place of J. R. Miller's "Practical
Gamekeeping.""

—Ed Zern, *Field and Stream* (Nov. 1959)

Hilary Price

"SAY, BABY—
'COME LIVE WITH ME AND BE MY LOVE,
AND WE WILL ALL THE PLEASURES PROVE,
THAT VALLEYS, GROVES, HILLS AND FIELDS,
WOODS OR STEEPY MOUNTAIN YIELDS.'
                              MARLOWE."

Sidney Harris

"This is not a novel to be tossed aside lightly. It should be thrown with great force."
—Dorothy Parker

"From the moment I picked up your book until I laid it down, I was convulsed with laughter. Some day I intend reading it."
—Groucho Marx

"I read part of the book all the way through."
—Samuel Goldwyn

"A person who won't read has no advantage over one who can't read."
—Mark Twain

A poor Talmud scholar approached his rabbi with his masterpiece: a commentary on the *Mishnah*.

"Better you should stop writing," said the rabbi. "It won't get you anywhere."

"And if I stopped writing," replied the scholar, "would it get me anywhere?"

"What an author likes to write most is his signature on the back of a cheque."
—Brendan Behan

"A bad review may spoil your breakfast, but you shouldn't allow it to spoil your lunch."
—Kingsley Amis

"Avez-vous 'Ulysses'?"

Helen E. Hokinson

"I'm sorry to bother you, but by any chance do you happen to have a copy of Baudelaire's *Les Fleurs du Mal* on your person?"

Christopher Burke

I used to be a structuralist, but now I'm not Saussure.

"Why did Jacques Derrida hate Christmas?
—Because of the absence of presence.

How do you know when you've been approached by the Deconstructivist Mafia?
—They make you an offer you can't understand.

A man walks into a bookshop and says, "Can I have a book by Shakespeare?"

"Of course, sir," says the salesman. "Which one?"

To which the man replies, "William."

A street beggar asks a gentleman if he can spare some change.

GENTLEMAN: "Neither a borrower nor a lender be." —William Shakespeare.

BEGGAR: "Fuck you!" —David Mamet.

A Shakespearean actor goes to a brothel. Once in the room with his lady of choice, he pulls down his pants. She whistles and says, "My... that's a big one!"

"Madam," says the actor, "we've come to bury Caesar, not to praise him."

Actual footnote to the expression "country matters" in a school edition of *Hamlet*.
— "Emphasis on the first syllable."

"Godot says, 'Running late, frowny face, winky face.' "

Benjamin Schwartz

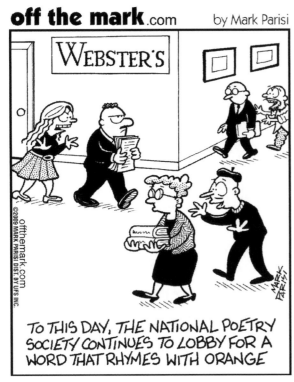

Mark Parisi

"A poet can survive everything but a misprint."
　　　—Oscar Wilde

A poetry teacher's critique of a student's work:

"Put more fire into your poems, or vice-versa."

W hat is a simile?
　　　—It's like a metaphor.

M etaphors be with you!

L.J. Kopf

The Introduction
by Billy Collins

I don't think this next poem
needs any introduction—
it's best to let the work speak for itself.

Maybe I should just mention
that whenever I use the word *five*,
I'm referring to that group of Russian composers
who came to be known as "The Five,"
Balakirev, Moussorgsky, Borodin—that crowd.

Oh—and Hypsicles was a Greek astronomer.
He did something with the circle.

That's about it, but for the record,
"Grimké" is Angelina Emily Grimké, the abolitionist.
"Imroz" is that little island near the Dardanelles.
'Monad"—well, you all know what a monad is.

There could be a little problem
with *mastaba*, which is one of those Egyptian
above-ground sepulchers, sort of brick and limestone.

And you're all familiar with helminthology?
It's the science of worms.

Oh, and you will recall that Phoebe Mozee
is the real name of Annie Oakley.

Other than that, everything should be obvious.
Wagga Wagga is in New South Wales.
Rhyolite is that soft volcanic rock.
What else?
Yes, *meranti* is a type of timber, in tropical Asia I think,
and Rahway is just Rahway, New Jersey.

The rest of the poem should be clear.
I'll just read it and let it speak for itself.

It's about the time I went picking wild strawberries.

It's called "Picking Wild Strawberries."

© Billy Collins. Reprinted with permission of Penguin Random House. All rights reserved.

How to Write Good

- Always avidly avoid alliteration.
- Never use a long word when a diminutive one will do.
- Employ the vernacular.
- Steer clear of ampersands & abbreviations, etc.
- Parenthetical remarks (however relevant) are unnecessary.
- Remember to never split an infinitive.
- Contractions aren't necessary.
- Foreign words and phrases are not à propos.
- One should never generalize.
- Eliminate quotations. As Ralph Waldo Emerson said, "I hate quotations. Tell me what you know."
- Don't be redundant; don't use more words than necessary; it's highly superfluous.
- Be more or less specific.
- Understatement is always best.
- Analogies in writing are like feathers on a snake.
- The passive voice is to be avoided.
- Even if a mixed metaphor sings, it should be derailed.
- Who needs rhetorical questions?
- Exaggeration is a billion times worse than understatement.
- Don't never use a double negative.
- Verbs has to agree with their subjects.
- Proofread carefully to see if you words out.
- If you reread your work, you can find on rereading a great deal of repetition can be avoided by rereading and editing.
- And never start a sentence with a conjunction.
- A preposition is a terrible word to end a sentence with.
- Writing carefully, dangling participles must be avoided.
- Everyone should be careful to use a singular pronoun with singular nouns in their writing.
- Always pick on the correct idiom.
- The adverb always follows the verb.
- Last but not least, avoid cliches like the plague.

"Substitute *damn* every time you're inclined to write *very*; your editor will delete it and the writing will be just as it should be."
—Mark Twain

Calvin and Hobbes

Panel 1: IF YOU ASK *ME*, THESE ASSIGNMENTS DON'T TEACH YOU HOW TO WRITE. THEY TEACH YOU HOW TO *HATE* TO WRITE.

Panel 2: DEADLINES, RULES HOW TO DO IT, GRADES... HOW CAN YOU BE CREATIVE WHEN SOMEONE'S BREATHING DOWN YOUR NECK?

Panel 3: I GUESS YOU SHOULD TRY NOT TO THINK ABOUT THE END RESULT TOO MUCH AND JUST HAVE FUN WITH THE PROCESS OF CREATING.

Panel 4: EVERY TIME I DO THAT, I END UP IN THE SCHOOL PSYCHOLOGIST'S OFFICE. | WELL, MAYBE NOT *THAT* MUCH FUN.

CALVIN AND HOBBES © 1992 Watterson. Reprinted with permission of UNIVERSAL UCLICK. All rights reserved.

Bill Watterson

An Infinite Number of Writers

A young man on vacation calls home and speaks to his brother. "How's my cat Oscar?"

"Cat's dead. Died this morning."

"That's terrible. You know how attached I was to Oscar."

"Yep."

"Couldn't you have broken the news more gently?"

"Huh? What do you mean?"

"You could've said the cat's up on the roof. Then the next time I called, you could have said that you haven't been able to get him down. And then the next time you could have said that the cat jumped down but is badly hurt. And gradually like this you could've broken the news."

"Okay, I see. Sorry."

"Anyway, how's mom?"

"She's up on the roof."

"O.K.—let's get our stories straight, and our characters sympathetic and well drawn."

Emily Flake

"I write when I'm inspired, and I see to it that I'm inspired at nine o'clock every morning."
　　　—Peter De Vries

"It's no wonder that truth is stranger than fiction. Fiction, after all, has to make sense."
　　　—Mark Twain

"I'm not a very good writer, but I'm an excellent rewriter."
　　　—James Michener

The covers of this book are too far apart.

In every fat book there's a thin book trying to get out.

"No caffè latte? And you call yourselves a bookstore?"

Danny Shanahan

"There's not much to be said about the period except that most writers don't reach it soon enough."
　　　—William Zinsser

Hilary Price

TOP 10 BOOKSTORE PICKUP LINES

10. Care to come back to my place for a little Dickens?

9. When you're tired of dating "speed readers" —call me.

8. You're pretty nicely stacked yourself.

7. Have you seen a copy of *Tax Tips for Billionaires*?

6. Who's your favorite Karamazov brother?

5. I've got a great reading light next to my bed.

4. I can bench-press a whole stack of James Michener novels.

3. While you're turning those pages, mind if I lick your fingers?

2. You're hotter than Emily Dickinson in a tube top.

1. Is that an unabridged dictionary in your pocket, or are you just glad to see me?

Old librarians don't die, they just get reclassified.

MARY, TO TOM: That's a great collection of books you've got there. But why are they on the floor? You ought to put up some shelves.

TOM: I would, but no one wants to lend me shelves.

Dave Coverly

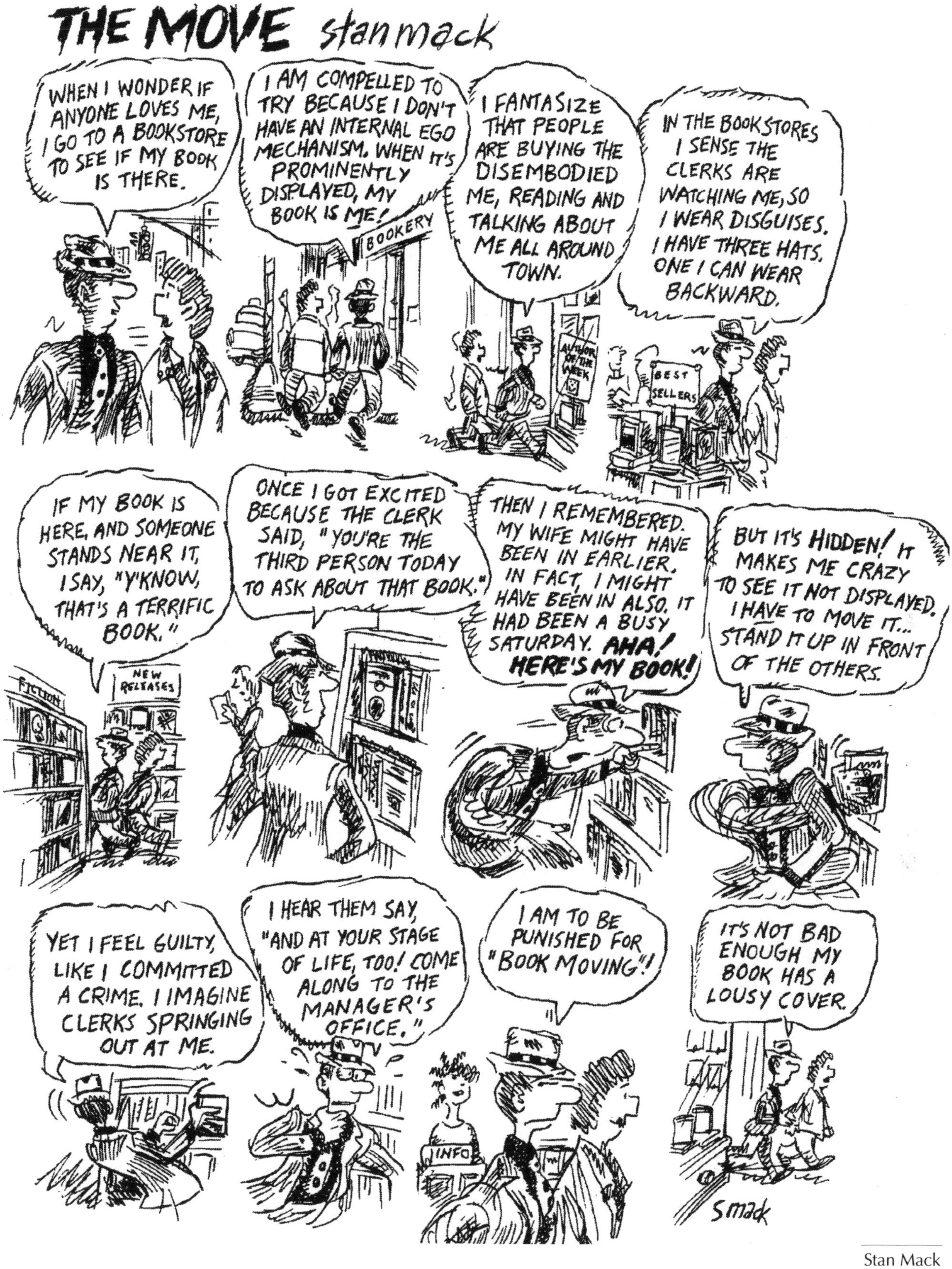
THE MOVE stanmack
WHEN I WONDER IF ANYONE LOVES ME, I GO TO A BOOKSTORE TO SEE IF MY BOOK IS THERE.
I AM COMPELLED TO TRY BECAUSE I DON'T HAVE AN INTERNAL EGO MECHANISM. WHEN IT'S PROMINENTLY DISPLAYED, MY BOOK IS ME!
BOOKERY
I FANTASIZE THAT PEOPLE ARE BUYING THE DISEMBODIED ME, READING AND TALKING ABOUT ME ALL AROUND TOWN.
AUTHOR OF THE WEEK
IN THE BOOKSTORES I SENSE THE CLERKS ARE WATCHING ME, SO I WEAR DISGUISES. I HAVE THREE HATS. ONE I CAN WEAR BACKWARD.
BEST SELLERS
IF MY BOOK IS HERE, AND SOMEONE STANDS NEAR IT, I SAY, "Y'KNOW, THAT'S A TERRIFIC BOOK."
FICTION
NEW RELEASES
ONCE I GOT EXCITED BECAUSE THE CLERK SAID, "YOU'RE THE THIRD PERSON TODAY TO ASK ABOUT THAT BOOK."
THEN I REMEMBERED. MY WIFE MIGHT HAVE BEEN IN EARLIER. IN FACT, I MIGHT HAVE BEEN IN ALSO. IT HAD BEEN A BUSY SATURDAY. AHA! HERE'S MY BOOK!
BUT IT'S HIDDEN! IT MAKES ME CRAZY TO SEE IT NOT DISPLAYED. I HAVE TO MOVE IT... STAND IT UP IN FRONT OF THE OTHERS.
YET I FEEL GUILTY, LIKE I COMMITTED A CRIME. I IMAGINE CLERKS SPRINGING OUT AT ME.
I HEAR THEM SAY, "AND AT YOUR STAGE OF LIFE, TOO! COME ALONG TO THE MANAGER'S OFFICE."
INFO
I AM TO BE PUNISHED FOR "BOOK MOVING"!
IT'S NOT BAD ENOUGH MY BOOK HAS A LOUSY COVER.
SMACK

Stan Mack

"I can write better than anybody who can write faster, and I can write faster than anybody who can write better."
—A. J. Liebling

"It took me fifteen years to discover that I had no talent for writing, but I couldn't give it up because by that time I was too famous."
—Robert Benchley

"I love being a writer. What I can't stand is the paperwork."
—Peter De Vries

Dr. Samuel Johnson, to an aspiring writer: "Your manuscript is both good and original; but the part that is good is not original, and the part that is original is not good."

"Having been unpopular in high school is not just cause for book publication."
—Fran Lebowitz

"Everywhere I go I'm asked if I think the university stifles writers. My opinion is that they don't stifle enough of them. There's many a best-seller that could have been prevented by a good teacher."
—Flannery O'Connor

"Always read something that will make you look good if you die in the middle of it."
—P.J. O'Rourke

"A classic is something that everybody wants to have read and nobody wants to read."
—Mark Twain

"Outside of a dog, a book is a man's best friend. Inside of a dog it's too dark to read."
—Groucho Marx

"Why, you're right. Tonight isn't reading night, tonight is sex night."

Robert Mankoff

148

Bradford Veley

You can trust me. = *You must be new.*

It needs some polishing. = *Change everything.*

It shows promise. = *It stinks rotten.*

It needs some fine tuning. = *Change everything.*

I'd like some input. = *I want total control.*

It needs some honing. = *Change everything.*

Call me back next week. = *Stay out of my life.*

It needs some tightening. = *Change everything.*

Try and punch it up. = *I have no idea what I want.*

It needs some streamlining. = *Change everything.*

You'll never work in this town again. = *I have no power whatsoever.*

Two movie development execs meet in the hallway. One says, "Hey, what's cooking?"

The second one, extremely excited, replies, "I just bought this script. It's the most brilliant piece of writing I've ever seen. Characters, story, everything about it is A-Number-One! Academy Award time!!"

"That's fantastic," says the first one, dripping with envy. "So when do you go into production?"

"As soon as I get the rewrite."

Did you hear about the ambitious starlet who had no clue?

—She slept with the screenwriter.

"Every novel should have a beginning, a muddle, and an end."

—Peter DeVries

"Boy meets girl; girl gets boy into pickle; boy gets pickle into girl."

—Jack Woodford

"Writers seldom write the things they think. They simply write the things they think other people think they think."

—Elbert Hubbard

"It starts out with a standard romantic plot: Boy meets Girl, Boy loses Girl, wins her back, Girl kills Boy, devours his head and lays eggs in his carcass. OK, now here's the twist..."

Bradford Veley

THE RULES OF SCREENWRITING

- During all police investigations, it will be necessary to visit a strip club at least once.

- If being chased through town, you must always take cover in a passing parade —at any time of the year.

- If your gun runs out of ammunition, throw it away. No one ever carries extra bullets with them.

- The ventilation system of any building makes a perfect hiding place. No one will ever think of looking for you in there, and you can travel to any other part of the building without difficulty.

- A man should show no pain while taking the most ferocious beating, but should wince when a woman tries to clean his wounds.

- Cars that crash must always burst into flames.

- You can always find a chain saw when you need one.

- Any triple-locked door can be broken down with one swift kick.

- The Chief of Police must either suspend his star detective or give him 48 hours to finish the job.

- All bombs must be fitted with electronic timing devices with large red readouts so you know exactly when they're going to go off.

- Any lock can be picked by a credit card or a paper clip in seconds —unless it's the door to a burning building with a child trapped inside.

- Police departments must give their officers personality tests to make sure they are deliberately assigned a partner who is their total opposite.

- When a person is knocked unconscious by a blow to the head, they must never suffer a concussion or brain damage or go into shock.

- It doesn't matter if you are heavily outnumbered in a fight involving martial arts —your enemies must wait patiently to attack you one by one.

- Should you wish to pass yourself off as a German officer, it will not be necessary to speak the language —a bad German accent will do.

- You can survive any battle in any war, unless you make the mistake of showing someone a picture of your sweetheart back home.

- All grocery shopping bags must contain at least one loaf of French bread or bunch of celery that sticks out the top. If the bag is dropped, a dozen eggs and several oranges must roll out of it.

- If you're sitting on a park bench minding your own business, a lot of crows will gather behind you.

- If you take a shower, you will die.

- If you're hanging from Mt. Rushmore, your coiffure will stay in place.

- If you find yourself alone in the middle of nowhere, a crop duster must try to kill you.

- All beds must come with special L-shaped sheets which reach up to the armpit level on a woman but only to waist level on the man lying beside her.

- If two co-workers want to have sex, a desk in a busy office is the best place, provided that they are separated from their fellow employees by a wall of lightly frosted glass, which is always soundproof and opaque.

"Here's the kicker; after eating the grandma, he puts on her clothes, gets into bed, and waits for the girl to arrive..."

© MARK ANDERSON, WWW.ANDERTOONS.COM

Mark Anderson

"I've got an idea for a story: Gus and Ethel live on Long Island, on the North Shore. He works sixteen hours a day writing fiction. Ethel never goes out, never does anything except fix Gus sandwiches and in the end she becomes a nympho-lesbo-killer-whore. Here's your sandwich."

George Booth

"Practically everybody in New York has half a mind to write a book, and does."
—Groucho Marx

"I love deadlines. I love the whooshing noise they make as they go by."
—Douglas Adams

"Finish it? Why would I want to finish it?"

W.B. Park

Jim Anderson was a writer who was on the edge of disaster. He had written nothing in years that was any good and he had become an alcoholic. His apartment had nothing in it but a typewriter, a table on which it rested, a chair, and, in a second room, a bed.

One night, as he lay on his bed in an alcoholic daze and was thinking he would have to hock his typewriter, he heard a steady tap-tapping from the other room, as though someone were using his typewriter. He was too far gone in his stupor to check —so he fell asleep.

The next morning he found next to his typewriter a professionally formatted, beautifully typed movie script. He looked it over and was electrified by its extraordinary quality. It was much better than anything he could ever have written. He brought it to his agent, who, with the greatest reluctance, consented to glance at it. The agent was caught up at once.

"Jim," he said, "this is great. I don't know how you did it, but I'm sure I can sell it."

And sell it he did —for a large sum.

Thereafter, Anderson periodically heard the tap-tapping of the typewriter, periodically found another great script, periodically sold it for increasing sums of money. He grew rich and famous and lived in a wonderful mansion overlooking the ocean with everything his heart could possibly desire. In his new quarters, scripts continued to be turned out by his mysterious benefactor. But by now his curiosity overwhelmed him. Who was writing these scripts for him?

One night when he heard the tap-tapping, he sneaked into his study, and there at the typewriter was an elf in pointed hat, pointed shoes, the whole works. Said Anderson, "Have you been writing these scripts?"

"That I have," said the elf.

"But why?" asked Anderson.

"Because I love to," said the elf.

Anderson said, "Do you realize what you have done for me? I was on the point of suicide and you have made me rich and famous and happy and I'll soon be married to the most gorgeous woman in the world. Is there nothing I can do for you in exchange?"

"It's not necessary," said the elf. "I'm happy, too."

"But let me give you something: a house, a yacht, anything your heart desires. Anything. Anything."

"In that case," said the elf, "there is something. Can you put my name down as co-author on one of these scripts?"

And Anderson said, "Co-author!? Fuck you!"

GRAPES OF WRATH

"Tom Joad leaned down and untied the laces of his new yellow **NIKE AIR JORDANS,** slipped off first one shoe and..."

CRIME + PUNISHMENT

"Raskolnikov got **NEW DIAL DEODORANT** soap from Nastasya and washed his hair, his neck and with especial pains, his hands."

OLD MAN & THE SEA

"...Santiago said aloud, 'I can lash my **GINSU** knife to the butt of one of my **COLEMAN** oars."

EMILY DICKINSON

"...Again the smoke from **MARLBOROS** rose The Day abroad was heard How intimate, a Tempest past The Transport of the Bird."

SINGER

Andy Singer

Hilary Price

Writing a limerick's absurd,
    Line one and line five rhyme in word,
        And just as you've reckoned
        They rhyme with the second;
    But the fourth must rhyme with the
    third.

There was a young man of Japan
    Whose limericks never would scan.
        When asked why this was,
        He replied "It's because
    I always try to fit as many syllables into
    the last line as ever I possibly can."

There's a notable family named Stein,
    There's Gertrude, there's Ep, and there's
    Ein.
        Gert's prose is the bunk,
        Ep's sculpture is junk,
    And no one can understand Ein.

A publisher once went to France
    In search of a tale of romance
        A Parisian lady
        Told a story so shady
    That the publisher made an advance.

For years a secret shame destroyed my
    peace—
    I'd not read Eliot, Auden or MacNeice.
    But now I think a thought that brings
    me hope:
    Neither had Chaucer, Shakespeare,
    Milton, Pope.
        —Justin Richardson.

For those of you who don't know the
    difference between prose and poetry,
here is an explanation:
There was a young lady from Glass,
She went into the water up to her knees...
That's prose.
If she had gone any deeper, it would have
been poetry.

off the mark .com   by Mark Parisi

YOU ACCIDENTALLY SWITCHED THE SUPERGLUE AND THE PREPARATION H? WHAT HAPPENED?!

IT WAS CRAZY! MY COLLAGE WOULDN'T STICK!

offthemark.com
©2006 MARK PARISI DIST. BY UFS INC.

STORY LETDOWN

Mark Parisi

A Jewish gentleman is eating his lunch in the park when a blind man sits down next to him. He offers him a piece of matzoh.

The blind man takes it, fingers it for a moment, and then says "Who wrote this crap?"

"I'm writing a book. I've got the page numbers done, so now I just have to fill in the rest."
—Steven Wright

Why did Cormac McCarthy cross the road?
—Because he wrote it.

Why did they ban *Ivanhoe*?
—Too much Saxon violence.

What makes *Civil Disobedience* such a great essay?
—Thoreau editing.

If Voltaire were alive today: "I disapprove of your t-shirt, but I will defend to the death your right to wear it."

Do you like Kipling?
— I don't know. I've never kipled.

There was once a young man who, in his youth, professed his desire to become a great writer. When asked to define *great*, he said, "I want to write stuff that the whole world will read, stuff that people will react to on a truly emotional level, stuff that will make them scream, cry, howl in pain and anger!"

He now works for Microsoft writing error messages.

"Yes, I've read *Gulliver's Travels*," replied Tom swiftly.
• "This isn't the best of all possible worlds," said Tom candidly.
• "I'm having an affair with my gamekeeper," said the lady chattily.
• "Who stole the last chapter from my book of fables?" asked Tom, demoralized.
• "This is how I murdered the mystery writer," Tom described.
• "Do I really have to read another thick novel by Hugo?" asked Les miserably.
• "My next novel will be the greatest thing since *Finnegans Wake*," Tom rejoiced.
• "I saw the best minds of my generation destroyed by madness!" Tom howled.

How many writers does it take to change a lightbulb?

—But why do we have to change it?

- How many mystery writers does it take to screw in a lightbulb?

—Two, one to screw it almost all the way in and the other to give it a surprising twist at the end.

- How many science fiction writers does it take to screw in a lightbulb?

—Two, but you see it's actually the same person doing it. He went back in time and met himself crossing through a portal, and then the first one sat on the other one's shoulder so that they were able to reach the bulb. Then a major time paradox occurred and the entire room —lightbulb, changer, and all— was blown out of existence. They continued to co-exist in a parallel universe, however.

- How many male novelists does it take to screw in a lightbulb?

—The time had come for him to go to war, to find himself, to forever reject the rules of your society.

- How many poets does it take to change a lightbulb?

—Three. One to curse the darkness, one to light a candle... ... and one to change the bulb.

- How many screenwriters does it take to change a lightbulb?

—Ten:

1st draft. Hero changes lightbulb.
2nd draft. Villain changes lightbulb.
3rd draft. Hero stops villain from changing lightbulb. Villain falls to death.
4th draft. Lose the lightbulb.
5th draft. Lightbulb back in. Fluorescent instead of tungsten.
6th draft. Villain breaks bulb, uses it to kill hero's mentor.
7th draft. Fluorescent not working. Back to tungsten.
8th draft. Hero forces villain to eat lightbulb.
9th draft. Hero laments loss of lightbulb. Doesn't change it.
10th draft. Hero changes lightbulb.

- How many librarians does it take to screw in a lightbulb?

—I don't know, but I can look it up for you.

- How many editors does it take to screw in a lightbulb?

—Two. One to change the bulb and one to issue a rejection slip to the old bulb.

- How many booksellers does it take to screw in a lightbulb?

—Only one, and they'd be glad to do it too, except no one shipped them any.

- How many reviewers does it take to screw in a lightbulb?

—None. They just stand back and critique while you do all the work.

- How many publishers does it take to screw in a lightbulb?

—Three. One to screw it in. Two to hold down the author.

Chapter Eight

A π in the Face

Just Do the Math

Loren Fishman

Andy Singer

Why did the chicken cross the Möbius strip?
—To get to the same side.

To be or not to be, that is the question.
—No, 2B *or* not 2B is the answer. The question is: what is the square root of 4B^2?

At a Cal Tech seminar.
RICHARD FEYNMAN: If mathematics did not exist, it would set the world back one week.
MARK KAC: Precisely the week in which God created the world.

There was once a very brilliant horse who mastered arithmetic, algebra, plane geometry, and trigonometry. When presented with problems in analytic geometry, however, the horse would kick, neigh, and struggle desperately. One just couldn't put Descartes before the horse.

Three guys in a mental hospital are offered the chance to get out, if they can only answer one simple question: What is the square root of 9 times the square root of 16?
"A gazillion," says the first man.
"No, sorry," says the hospital administrator.
"Tuesday!" says the second.
"Close," says the administrator wryly, "but sorry, no."
Finally, he asks the third man.
The answer comes immediately: "The square root of 9 times the square root of 16? Easy. It's 12."
The administrator is impressed and tells him, okay, you can leave the hospital now. "By the way," he adds, "how the heck did you figure that out?"
"Simple," says the patient. "I just took a gazillion and divided by Tuesday."

Math is like love —a simple idea, but it can get complicated.

Mathematician: a device for turning coffee into theorems.

Mathematician to her misbehaving children: "If I've told you n times, I've told you n+1 times…"

Dear Algebra,
Stop asking us to find your X.
She's not coming back.
We don't know Y either.

Algebra is the intensive study of the last three letters of the alphabet.

Without geometry, life is pointless.

A π in the Face

The young couple was engaged in a most passionate embrace when there came the sound of a key in the front door. The young lady broke away at once, eyes wide with alarm. "Heavens," she cried, "it's my husband! Quick, jump out the window."

The young man, equally alarmed, made a quick step toward the window, then hesitated. "I can't," he said, "we're on the 13th floor."

"For heaven's sake," cried the young lady in exasperation, "this is no time to be superstitious."

Waldo asked his doctor how to improve his relationship with his wife. The doctor advised him to take a 10-mile bike ride each night so he wouldn't be so irritable, and to call him in a month. When Waldo called the next month, the doctor asked him how things were with his wife. "Fine, I'm very relaxed, but I'm 300 miles from home."

Dan Piraro

David Sipress

159

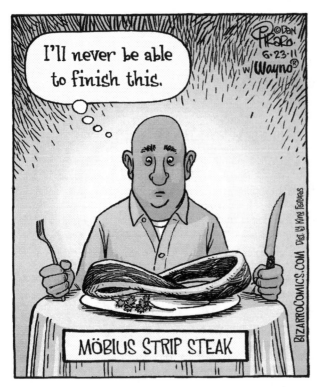

I'll never be able to finish this.

MÖBIUS STRIP STEAK

Dan Piraro

Walter, a very nervous man, has never flown on a plane before and is inordinately freaked out by the possibility of terrorism in the skies. But Walter is also a very loyal friend who has promised to go cross-country and back that weekend to be best man at his college roommate's wedding. Somehow he will do this.

He calls the airline and says, "I have to know I'll be safe. What is the probability that someone will bring a bomb onto the plane?"

The airline clerk answers, "Oh, the chances are very slim. It's about one in a million."

Walter says, "Well, I'm still not so sure. Tell me, what are the chances of there being two people bringing bombs on the plane?"

The airline clerk replies, "Oh, that's even slimmer. It's like one in ten million."

Walter says, "Oh, that's better. In that case I'd like to book a flight for tomorrow night."

The next night Walter boards the plane and brings a bomb with him.

A math teacher is having trouble with his sink, so he calls a plumber. The plumber comes over and quickly fixes it. The teacher is delighted until the plumber gives him the bill. "Do you know how long I have to work to make that kind of money?" he protests. But he pays the bill.

The plumber says to him, "I understand your position as a teacher. Why don't you come to our company and apply for a job as a plumber? You'll earn three times as much as you do as a math teacher. But remember, when you apply, tell them you're a high school dropout. They don't like educated people."

And so he does. The teacher gets a job as a plumber and his life significantly improves. His salary triples and he doesn't have to work nearly as hard.

One day, the plumbing company gets taken over by new, more "modern" management, whose policy it is that every plumber has to go to evening classes to complete high school. Of course our teacher has to go there too. And it just so happens that the first class is math.

The instructor, to check the students' knowledge, asks for the formula for the area of a circle. The first person called on is none other than our former math teacher. He jumps to the board, but then has a bad case of nerves and blanks on the formula.

Reverting to mathematician mode, he tries to derive it and is soon filling the board with integrals, differentials, and other advanced formulas. He ends up figuring out that it's "negative pi times r squared." But he knows the negative must be wrong, so he starts all over again. Again he gets the negative sign.

No matter how many times he tries, he always gets a negative. Frustrated, he looks nervously at the class and sees that all the other plumbers are whispering, "Switch the limits of the integral!"

A π in the Face

"I think he's trying to tell us something."

© MARK ANDERSON, WWW.ANDERTOONS.COM

Mark Anderson

One of the greatest moments in a mathematician's life is right after proving a result but before finding a mistake.

A mathematician goes to the zoo and carefully positions himself close enough to one of the camels so he can drop a straw squarely on its back.

The camel turns his head and says, "Wrong straw."

A Roman walks into a bar, holds up two fingers, and says "Five beers, please."

Mark Parisi

A π in the Face

CALVIN AND HOBBES © 1990 Watterson. Reprinted with permission of UNIVERSAL UCLICK. All rights reserved.

Bill Watterson

Jack Ziegler

An immigrant who had worked his way up from poverty was very proud of his scientist son at Harvard. On a visit home during his freshman year, the young man could not hide his excitement about his latest studies: Einstein's theory of relativity. His father asked him to explain it.

After some thought as to how to translate it into layman's language, the son said "Relativity is like this: If you're sitting on a hot stove, a minute seems like an hour. If you're in bed with a beautiful, naked woman, an hour goes by like a minute. It's all relative."

The old man thought about this and scratched his head: "And from this your Mr. Einstein makes a living?"

A student traveling by train from Boston to Princeton recognizes Einstein on board and asks him: "Excuse me, professor, but does New York stop at this train?"

During Einstein's tenure as a professor at Princeton, one of his students came up to him and said: "The questions on this year's exam are the same as last year's!"

"True," Einstein said, "but this year all the answers are different."

Once when Einstein was in Hollywood on a visit, Charlie Chaplin drove him through the town. As the people on the sidewalks recognized two of their greatest, if very different, contemporaries, they gave them a tremendous reception, which greatly astonished Einstein.

"They're cheering us both," said Chaplin, "you because nobody understands you, and me because everybody understands me."

EINSTEIN PONDERS THE MYSTERIES OF SPACE AND TIME

Robert Leighton

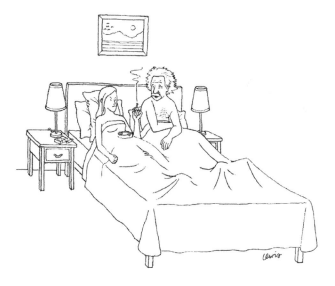

"To you it was fast."

Eric Lewis

*"Of course, the real charm of the place is that
hole in the space-time continuum."*

Tom Cheney

"Professor," said the student in search of knowledge, "can you explain to me the theory of limits?"

"Well, young man, let's assume that you are lucky enough to find yourself alone with a pretty young woman who, shall we say, you are trying to get to know better. You are seated at one end of the sofa and she is seated at the other end. You move half way toward her. Then you move half of the remaining distance toward her. And again you reduce the distance separating you from her by fifty percent. You continue this for some time. Theoretically you will never reach her. On the other hand, you will get close enough for all practical purposes."

Zeno walks halfway into a bar. The bartender keeps telling him to come closer. Zeno dies of thirst.

Francis Acupan

A π in the Face

Calvin and Hobbes

PLAYING A RECORD? I'LL SHOW YOU SOMETHING INTERESTING.

COMPARE A POINT ON THE LABEL WITH A POINT ON THE RECORD'S OUTER EDGE. THEY BOTH MAKE A COMPLETE CIRCLE IN THE SAME AMOUNT OF TIME, RIGHT?

YEAH...

BUT THE POINT ON THE RECORD'S EDGE HAS TO MAKE A BIGGER CIRCLE IN THE SAME TIME, SO IT GOES FASTER. SEE, TWO POINTS ON ONE DISK MOVE AT TWO SPEEDS, EVEN THOUGH THEY BOTH MAKE THE SAME REVOLUTIONS PER MINUTE!

CALVIN AND HOBBES © 1990 Watterson. Reprinted with permission of UNIVERSAL UCLICK. All rights reserved.

Bill Watterson

One day an acclaimed mathematician decides that his life, though in many ways successful, lacks adventure. As a child, he had always dreamed of becoming a fireman, and since there's no time like the present, he walks into his town's volunteer firehouse and offers his services.

The fire chief says, "We'd be glad to have you, but first I am required to give you a little test. Just a formality, an insult to your intelligence really, but it's regulations."

And this is how the mathematician flunked the test:

The fire chief takes him to the alley behind the firehouse, where there's a dumpster, a spigot, and a hose. The chief then says, "OK, you're walking in the alley and you see the dumpster here is on fire. What do you do?"

The mathematician replies, "Easy. I hook up the hose to the spigot, turn the water on, and put out the fire."

The chief says, "Correct. Now, what do you do if you're walking down the alley and you see the dumpster is not on fire?"

The mathematician puzzles over the question for a bit and then says, "I light the dumpster on fire."

The chief yells, "What? That's insane! Why would you light the dumpster on fire?"

The mathematician replies, "Well, that way I reduce the problem to one I've already solved."

A mathematician wandered home at 3 a.m. His wife was very upset, and yelled at him, "You're late! You said you'd be home by 11:45!"

The mathematician replied, "I'm right on time. I said I'd be home by a quarter of twelve."

The Flood is over and the ark has landed. Noah lets all the animals out and says, "Go forth and multiply."

A few months later, Noah decides to take a stroll and see how the animals are doing. Everywhere he looks he finds baby animals. Everyone is thriving except for one pair of little snakes. "What's the problem?" asks Noah.

"Cut down some trees and let us live there," say the snakes.

Noah follows their advice. Several more weeks pass. Noah checks on the snakes again. Lots of little snakes. Everybody is happy. Noah asks, "Want to tell me how the trees helped?"

"Certainly," say the snakes. "We're adders, so we need logs to multiply."

What does the "B" in Benoit B. Mandelbrot stand for?

—Benoit B. Mandelbrot

Dan Piraro

Did you hear about the mathematician who loved his wife so much that he almost told her?

An engineer, a physicist, and a mathematician are all in their labs when a fire breaks out in the building, spreading to each of their labs..

The engineer quickly grabs a fire hose, floods his lab with water, and puts the fire out, but in the process destroys all the equipment.

The physicist gets a glass of water, a piece of paper, and a pencil, and proceeds to calculate the critical point of the fire. He then throws the glass of water on the critical point and the whole fire goes out. His lab is saved.

The mathematician gets a glass of water, a piece of paper, and a match. He then sets the piece of paper on fire with the match, drops it in the water, and sees it go out. "Aha!" he exclaims. "A solution exists!"

A math student who usually comes to the university on foot arrives one morning on a shiny new bicycle. "Where did you get the bike from?" his fellow math geeks want to know.

"It's a thank-you present," he explains, "from that freshman girl I've been tutoring. But the story is kind of weird…"

"So tell us already!"

"Well," he starts, "yesterday she phoned and was very excited to tell me that she had passed her math final and that she wanted to drop by to thank me in person. She arrived at my place riding a brand-new bike. But when I let her in, she suddenly took off all her clothes, lay down on my bed, gave me a big smile, and said: `You can get from me whatever you desire!'"

One of his friends remarks: "You made a really smart choice when you took the bicycle."

"Yeah", another friend adds, "just imagine how silly you would have looked in that girl's clothes —and they wouldn't have fit you anyway."

Three logicians walk into a bar. The bartender asks "Do all of you want a drink?" The first logician says "I don't know." The second logician says the same. The third says "Yes!"

$$\frac{\sin x}{n} = ?$$

$$\frac{si\cancel{n}x}{\cancel{n}} = Six = 6$$

A π in the Face

USEFUL METRIC CONVERSIONS

2 monograms = 1 diagram

8 nickels = 2 paradigms

2 baby sitters = 1 gramma grampa

2,000 pounds of Chinese soup = Won ton

2,000 mockingbirds = two kilomockingbirds

1 million microphones = 1 megaphone

1 million bicycles = 2 megacycles

10 cards = 1 decacards

½ lavatory = 1 demijohn

1 millionth of a fish = 1 microfiche

453.6 graham crackers = 1 pound cake

10 rations = 1 decoration

10 millipedes = 1 centipede

10 monologs = 5 dialogues

1 millionth of a mouthwash = 1 microscope

365.25 days of drinking low-calorie beer because it's less filling = 1 lite year

1000 cubic centimeters of wet socks = 1 literhosen

16.5 feet in the Twilight Zone = 1 rod serling

1000 aches = 1 kilohurtz

Weight an evangelist carries with God = 1 billigram

3 statute miles of intravenous surgical tubing at Yale University Hospital = 1 I.V. league

Ratio of an igloo's circumference to its diameter = Eskimo Pi

Time between slipping on a peel and your head smacking the pavement = 1 bananosecond

"A billion is a thousand million? Why wasn't I informed of this?"

Robert Mankoff

167

Larry and David, both mathematicians, are having a friendly debate over beers at the local bar. Larry maintains that the average person knows very little about basic mathematics, while David takes the opposite position. When Larry goes off to the washroom, David calls over the blonde waitress. Promising her a generous tip, he tells her that when she delivers the check, he will ask her a question. All she has to do is answer "one third x cubed."

She repeats: "one thir dex cue?"

He corrects her: "one third x cubed."

She says, "one thir dex cupid?"

"Close enough," he says. So she agrees, and goes off mumbling to herself, "one thir dex cupid..."

Larry returns and David proposes the bet, saying he will ask the blonde waitress an integral. Larry confidently takes the bet. When the check arrives, David innocently asks her "what's the integral of x squared?"

The waitress says "one third x cubed" and while walking away, turns back and says over her shoulder "plus a constant."

"I didn't reach the same conclusion, Phil. In fact, my preliminary figures indicate we just can't go on meeting like this!"

Bradford Veley

Three statisticians go on a hunting expedition together. They spot a rabbit and the first statistician shoots at it, missing about a foot too far to the left. The second one then takes a shot, but he misses a foot to the right. The third statistician says, "Aha! Got it!"

Three leading economists take a small plane to the wilderness in northern Canada to hunt moose over the weekend. The last thing the pilot says is "Remember, this is a very small plane, so we can only bring ONE moose back."

But of course they kill one each and on Sunday they bribe the reluctant pilot into letting them bring all three dead moose onboard.

Bad idea: just after takeoff, the plane stalls and crashes. In the wreckage, the economists wake up, look around, and one of them says, "Where the hell are we?"

"Oh," says another, "just about a hundred yards east of the place where we crashed last year."

Economics is the only field in which two people can get a Nobel Prize for saying exactly the opposite thing.

Why did God create economists? —In order to make weather forecasters look good.

Two economists meet on the street. One inquires, "How's your wife?"
The other responds, "Relative to what?"

I asked an economist for her phone number....and she gave me an estimate.

$$E = \left[\frac{hc}{2\lambda}\right]_z + \left[2\left(\frac{\varepsilon_0 E^2}{4}\right)_Y \cos^2(\omega t) + \left(\frac{B^2}{2\mu_0}\right)_X \sin^2(\omega t)\right] v$$

$$E = \frac{\pi e}{\varepsilon_0 \alpha 3 \lambda^2} \quad B = \frac{\mu_0 \pi e c}{\alpha 3 \lambda^2} \quad V = \frac{0.23}{2\pi \lambda^2}$$

"There it is. You forgot to convert to dog years."

© MARK ANDERSON, WWW.ANDERTOONS.COM

Mark Anderson

A mathematician, an accountant and an economist apply for the same job.

The interviewer calls in the mathematician and asks "What does two plus two equal?"

The mathematician replies "Four."

The interviewer asks "Four, exactly?"

The mathematician looks at the interviewer incredulously and says "Yes, four, exactly."

Then the interviewer calls in the accountant and asks the same question, "What does two plus two equal?"

The accountant says "On average, four —give or take ten percent, but on average, four."

Then the interviewer calls in the economist and poses the same question, "What does two plus two equal?"

The economist gets up, locks the door, pulls the curtains, sits down real close to the interviewer, and whispers "What do you want it to equal?"

$$\left(\sqrt{-\text{shit}}\right)^2$$

...shit just got real

A History of Teaching Math

1950: A logger sells a truckload of lumber for $100. His cost of production is ⅘ of the price. What is his profit?

1960: A logger sells a truckload of lumber for $100. His cost of production is ⅘ of the price, or $80. What is his profit?

1970: A logger exchanges a set "L" of lumber for a set "M" of money. The cardinality of set "M" is 100. Each element is worth one dollar. Make 100 dots representing the elements of the set "M." The set "C", the cost of production, contains 20 fewer points than set "M." Represent the set "C" as a subset of set "M".

1980: By cutting down beautiful forest trees, the logger makes $20. What do you think of this way of making a living? Topic for discussion: how did the forest animals feel as the logger cut down the trees?

1990: A company outsources all of its loggers, saving on salaries and benefits, and when demand is down the work force can easily be cut back. The average logger previously employed by the company had earned $50,000, got 3 weeks vacation, and received medical insurance and a nice retirement plan. The contracted logger charges $50 an hour. Was outsourcing a good move?

2000: Enron sells a truckload of lumber for $500. The giant conglomerate's cost of production is $600. How does Arthur Andersen determine that Enron's profit margin is $300?

2010: By exporting its wood-finishing jobs to its Indonesian subsidiary, a logging company improves its stock price from $80 to $100. How much capital gain per share does the CEO make by exercising his stock options at $80 per share? Assume capital gains are no longer taxed, because this encourages investment.

2020: El hachero vende un camion carga por $700. La cuesta de production es............

Mark Parisi

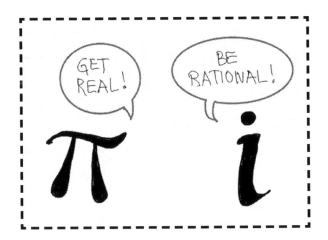

A π in the Face

WHATEVER YOU DO, DON'T TALK TO THAT GUY. HE'LL GO ON FOREVER

© 2008 By DOUG SAVAGE

PI IS THE LONELIEST NUMBER

Doug Savage

I thought it was a great idea to name our kid *Pi*, until the first time he misbehaved, and I realized I had to call him by his full name.

W hy do people get so excited about Pi Day?
—Who knows? It's completely irrational.

M y pin number is easy to remember. It's the last four digits of Pi.

T is a favorite project of mine
    A new value of pi to assign
        I would fix it at 3
        For it's simpler, you see,
Than 3 point 1-4-1-5-9.

S tatistics show that 3.14% of sailors are pirates.

T he roundest knight at King Arthur's court was Sir Cumference. Apparently he ate too much Pi.

T hree Navaho women sit side by side on the ground. The first woman, who is sitting on a buffalo skin, has a son who weighs 70 pounds. The second woman, who is sitting on a deer skin, has a son who weighs 80 pounds. The third woman, who weighs 150 pounds, is sitting on a hippopotamus skin.

The moral: the squaw of the hippopotamus is equal to the sons of the squaws of the other two hides.

B ack in 1970, Skip, a veteran air pilot, found his job threatened when a new type of commercial aircraft came on the market. It was necessary for all pilots, including Skip, to undergo a complete physical and psychological examination in order to make sure they were equipped to handle the new plane.

Skip passed the physical exam with flying colors, but next came the shrink, who asked him, "Tell me, sir, how long has it been since you have had a successful sexual experience with a woman?"

Skip's eyes narrowed and he said finally, "I should say it was about 1955."

The doctor looked startled. "That long ago. Isn't that unusual?"

Skip looked at his wristwatch. "Oh, I don't know. It's only 1105 now."

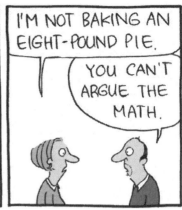

Hilary Price

How many eggs can you put into an empty basket?
—Only one. After that the basket isn't empty.

"We are sorry, but the number you have dialed is imaginary. Please rotate your phone 90° and try again."

Have you heard my new statistics joke?
—Probably.

"There are three kinds of lies: lies, damned lies, and statistics."
—Benjamin Disraeli

Statistics are like a bikini. What they reveal is suggestive. What they conceal is vital.

"People can come up with statistics to prove anything. Fourteen percent of people know that."
—Homer Simpson

Old mathematicians never die, they just lose some of their functions.

Geometry: What an acorn says when it's grown up.

What did zero say to eight?
—Nice belt!

Why was six afraid of seven?
—Because seven eight nine.

Think outside the quadrilateral parallelogram.

For a good prime, call 555-7523.

Did you hear what happened in the binary race?
—Zero one.

How do you make beer from root beer?
—Pour it into a square glass.

Why should the number 288 never be mentioned in polite company?
—Because it's two gross.

A π in the Face

W hy did the obtuse angle go to the beach?

—Because it was over 90°.

W hy don't they serve liquor at a math party?

—Because you can't drink and derive.

W hat do you get when you cross a mountain climber and a mosquito?

—Nothing! You can't cross a scalar and a vector.

T here are three kinds of people in this world:

People who can count and people who can't.

A mathematician named Hall
    Has a hexahedronical ball,
        And the cube of its weight
        Times his pecker, plus eight,
    Is his phone number —give him a call.

T here was a young lady named Bright
    Whose speed was faster than light
        She went out one day
        In a relative way,
    And returned the previous night.
    To her friends said the Bright one in chatter,
    "I have learned something new about matter:
        My speed was so great,
        Much increased was my weight.
    Yet I failed to become any fatter!"

"X is an integer," Tom declared.

• "There is no end to this sequence of digits," said Tom irrationally.
• "10, 20, 30, 40, 50..." said Tom intensely.
• "Add up this list of n numbers and then divide the sum by n," said Tom meanly.

• "Where's my book on the Taylor Series?" Tom asked summarily.
• "Next I will add all of the numbers," Tom said presumptuously.
• "That just doesn't add up," said Tom, nonplussed.
• "It has zero height, zero width, and —well, maybe I'll allow it to have a bit of depth," said Tom, stretching the point.
• "It's the quotient of two integers," said Tom rationally.
• "This value has to be converted to a floating point," Tom realized.
• "Must I show again why this theorem is true?" asked Tom reprovingly.

H ow many statisticians does it take to screw in a lightbulb?

—One, plus or minus three.
—On the average, one.

• How many Chicago School economists does it take to change a lightbulb?
—None. If the lightbulb needed changing the market would have already done it.

• How many chaos theorists does it take to screw in a lightbulb?
—None, they just get the butterfly to flap its wings a second time.

• How many mathematicians does it take to screw in a lightbulb?
—None. It's left to the reader as an exercise.
—A mathematician can't screw in a lightbulb, but he can easily prove the work can be done.
—One. He gives it to nine actors, thereby reducing the problem to a joke from chapter five.

Chapter Nine

It Takes Alkynes to Make a World

Mad About Science

"Scientists confirmed today that everything we know about the structure of the universe is wrongedy-wrong-wrong."

Jack Ziegler

Sidney Harris

A proton walks into a bar and says, "I'll have a martini with a cherry." The bartender says, "A cherry? Are you sure?" The proton replies, "Yes, I'm positive."

Next a cute red blood cell walks in and the proton asks "Care to join me at the bar?" The red cell answers, "Thank you but no, I'll just circulate."

Then a neutron walks in and asks how much the special is. The bartender replies, "For you, no charge."

After that, helium enters and tells a joke. The bartender says, "Don't make me laugh." Helium doesn't react.

Soon enough an oxygen atom walks in and says to the bartender "Quick, give me two hydrogen atoms, I'm really thirsty."

A minute later an atom of gold staggers in and picks a fight. The bartender sees him and yells, "Hey, you, get outta here!!" The atom of gold claims it wasn't his fault, but the bartender still kicks him out, muttering "Never trust an atom: they make up everything."

Last but certainly not least, a million neutrinos walk right into the bar. One of them says "Ouch!"

B ack in my day, we had *nine* planets.

"The sun, with all those planets revolving around it and dependent on it, can still ripen a bunch of grapes as if it had nothing else in the universe to do."
—Galileo Galilei

"If you wish to make an apple pie from scratch, you must first invent the universe."
—Carl Sagan

E ntropy sure ain't what it used to be.

G od @TheTweetOfGod
MISSING: One particle. Mass 125 GeV. Responds to name "Higgs." Somewhat small. If found, please return to Owner.
  Reward: Nobel Prize.
  —David Javerbaum,
  An Act of God

T he Higgs boson walks into a Catholic Church. The priest says, "What are you doing here?" HB says, "You can't have mass without me."

"It is now quite lawful for a Catholic woman to avoid pregnancy by a resort to mathematics, though she is still forbidden to resort to physics and chemistry."
—H.L. Mencken (1956)

It Takes Alkynes to Make a World

Cyanide & Happiness

"Physics is like sex. Sure, it may give some practical results, but that's not why we do it."
—Richard Feynman

Did you hear about the biologist who had twins?
—She baptized one and kept the other as a control.

Protesters in front of a physics lab:
"What do we want?"
"Time travel!!"
"When do we want it?"
"Irrelevant!!"

A photon arrives at the airport ticket counter and is asked if he has any bags to check. The photon answers, "No, I'm traveling light."

It Takes Alkynes to Make a World

Dan Piraro

"The good thing about science is that it's true whether or not you believe in it."
—Neil deGrasse Tyson

"Science: Ruining Everything Since 1543."
—Zach Weiner

"Copernicus, young man," said his parents to the lad at the age of twelve, "when are you going to come to terms with the fact that the world does not revolve around you?"

Biology is the only science in which multiplication is the same thing as division.

"The surest sign that intelligent life exists elsewhere in the universe is that it has never tried to contact us."
—Bill Watterson

It Takes Alkynes to Make a World

Hello, Police! I'd like to report a peeping anthropologist!

The big male senses danger and adopts a ritualized threatening posture.

Jane Goodall in the wilds of New Jersey.

Buddy Hickerson

I had an anthropology joke, but I realized that it didn't make sense in most cultural contexts.

An anthropologist walks into a bar and asks, "Why is this joke funny?"

What comprises the basic modern Navajo family unit?
—Mother, father, kids, grandma, and the anthropologist.

Sociology is the anthropology of white people.

"An archaeologist is the best husband a woman can have. The older she gets, the more interested he is in her."
—Agatha Christie

A biology professor was conducting research on the nervous system of the frog. Taking a frog out of the tank and putting it on the table, he said, "Jump!"

The frog jumped.

Taking a scalpel, he amputated one of the frog's legs. "Jump!" he shouted, and the frog jumped.

He amputated a hind leg. "Jump!" The frog managed a respectable jump.

Amputating a third limb, the professor repeated his command. Bleeding profusely by now, the frog managed a feeble bounce.

Taking the scalpel to the fourth leg, the professor said, "Jump!" No response from the frog.

"I said jump!" shouted the professor.

The frog didn't move.

"JUMP!!" he bellowed in the ear of the limbless animal. No movement whatsoever, and finally the scientist gave up, calling an end to the experiment.

Taking his notebook from the shelf, the biology professor carefully wrote down his conclusion: "When all limbs are amputated, it is observed that the frog goes deaf."

Wishing to teach his donkey not to eat, a pedant did not offer him any food. When the donkey died of hunger, he said, "I've had a great loss. Just when he had learned not to eat, he died."
—Hierokles & Philagrios (4th Century)

Mark Stivers

Pavlov is sitting at a pub enjoying a pint. The phone rings. He jumps up. He shouts, "Oh shit, I forgot to feed the dog!"

Bradford Veley

off the mark.com   by Mark Parisi

BELL RINGS, I GET A TREAT...
BELL RINGS, I GET A TREAT... IT
WENT ON THAT WAY FOR DAYS. THEN,
OUT OF THE BLUE ...BELL RINGS, I
GET **NOTHING AT ALL!!** NADA!
I MEAN, CAN YOU SERIOUSLY CALL
MY ATTACK UNPROVOKED?

THE DARK TRUTH ABOUT PAVLOV'S DOG.

Mark Parisi

Does the name Pavlov ring a bell?

"Pa, what's all this talk about Evolution?"

"Son, I'll have to consult my attorney before I can answer that question. I might be sent to jail for it."

Hanley (1925)

One day the zookeeper noticed that the orangutan was reading two books: *The Bible* and Darwin's *The Origin of Species*. Surprised, he asked the ape "Why are you reading both of those books?"

"Well," said the orangutan, "I'm just trying to figure out if I'm my brother's keeper or my keeper's brother."

Why did the dinosaur cross the road?
—Chickens hadn't evolved yet.

The nuclear war has come and gone. Earth lies devastated and nearly lifeless. In a puddle of water are two tiny bacteria. One says to the other, "Here we go again, but this time —no brains!"

Genetics explains why you look like your father and, if you don't, why you should.

"What I like about Mr. Darwin is that he tells it like it is."

Francis Acupan

"Evolution's been good to you, Sid."

Lee Lorenz

E volution is God's way of issuing upgrades.

"A hen is only an egg's way of making another egg."
—Samuel Butler (1877)

"P eople are DNA's way of making more DNA."
—Edward O. Wilson (1975)

A tourist at the Museum of Natural History asks a guard how old the dinosaur bones are. "100 million and four years old," the guard replies.

The tourist is dumbfounded. "100 million and four? How can you possibly know that?"

"Well," says the guard, "they were 100 million years old when I started working here four years ago."

A biologist is only a lab rat's way of making another lab rat.

"J ust to settle it once and for all: Which came first, the chicken or the egg? The egg —laid by a bird that was not a chicken."
—Neil deGrasse Tyson

Dave Coverly

Mark Parisi

Dan Piraro

Dan Piraro

Jeff Hobbs

It Takes Alkynes to Make a World   183

"I'd like to thank all those who made it
possible for me to be here tonight."

John Callahan

Peter Mueller

A man walks into a hotel, goes to the front desk and says: "Hello. I have a reservation. The name is Heisenberg."

The desk clerk responds: "Are you certain about that?"

Schrödinger's cat walks into a bar, and doesn't.

The Heineken Uncertainty Principle: "You can never be sure how many beers you had last night."

Heisenberg is driving Shrödinger to work when a cop pulls them over and asks Heisenberg, "Do you know how fast you were going?"

"No," replies Heisenberg, "but I know where I am."

The cop takes Heisenberg's license away from him so now Shrödinger has to drive, but a short while later another cop pulls over Schrödinger and asks him to open the car trunk. The cop looks in the trunk, and says, "Sir, do you know there's a dead cat in your trunk?"

"There is now," Schrödinger angrily replies.

Actually, Heisenberg hated driving cars. Every time he looked at the speedometer, he got lost.

Einstein, Newton and Pascal decide to play hide and seek. Einstein is it, so he closes his eyes, counts to 10, then opens them.

Pascal is nowhere to be seen, but Newton is right in front of Einstein, a piece of chalk in his hand. He is sitting in a box drawn in chalk on the ground, each side about a meter long.

Einstein says "Isaac, you're terrible at this. I found you right away!"

Newton says "No, no, Albert. You found one Newton per square meter. You found Pascal!"

Clive Goddard

I asked the librarian for a book about Pavlov's dogs and Schrödinger's cat. She said it rang a bell but she didn't know if it was there or not.

Zach Kanin

How do you prove that all odd numbers are prime?

MATHEMATICIAN: 3 is prime, 5 is prime, 7 is prime, the rest is seen by induction.

PHYSICIST: 3 is prime, 5 is prime, 7 is prime, 9 is experimental error, 11 is prime, 13 is prime, 15 is experimental error, 17 is prime, 19 is prime. The empirical evidence is overwhelming.

ENGINEER: 3 is prime, 5 is prime, 7 is prime, 9 is a good approximation, 11 is prime...

CREATIONIST : 3 is prime, 5 is prime, 7 is prime, 9 is prime.........

There are two kinds of scientific fact — those that support your views 100% and those that are very difficult to interpret.

A mathematician, a physicist, and an engineer are standing around a flag pole, looking up and debating what would be the best way to measure the pole's height. A social scientist walks by and asks them what they're doing.

Told what the challenge is, the social scientist loosens the bolts from the pole, knocks it over, measures it, and declares that it's 20 meters. The physicist laughs and says: "Typical social scientist. We wanted to know the height of the pole and he told us the width."

It Takes Alkynes to Make a World

An American scientist once visited the offices of the great Nobel Prize-winning physicist, Niels Bohr, in Copenhagen, and was amazed to find that over his desk was a horseshoe, securely nailed to the wall, with the open end up in the approved manner — so it would catch the good luck and not let it spill out.

The American said with a nervous laugh, "Surely you don't believe the horseshoe will bring you good luck, do you, Professor Bohr? After all, as a level-headed scientist…"

Bohr chuckled. "I believe no such thing, my good friend. Not at all. I am scarcely likely to believe in such foolish nonsense. However, I am told that a horseshoe will bring you good luck whether you believe in it or not."

How can you spot the topologists in the faculty cafeteria?
—They're the ones who can't tell their donuts from their coffee mugs.

It has been discovered that research causes cancer in laboratory rats.

What does the "H" in Jesus H. Christ stand for?
—"Haploid"

Why did the tachyon cross the road?
—Because it was already on the other side.

An unknown sub-atomic particle waiting to be discovered.

Bradford Veley

187

Speech bubble (left): Remember how I used to beat you up in school & call you a "science nerd"? Ironic, huh?

Speech bubble (right): And you may experience further irony during your colonoscopy tomorrow, too.

Dan Piraro

E very Friday afternoon, a theoretical physicist goes down to the corner bar, sits in the second-to-last seat, turns to the last seat, which is empty, and asks a girl who isn't there if he can buy her a drink. The bartender, who is used to weird university types, always shrugs but keeps quiet. But when Valentine's Day arrives, and the man makes a particularly heart-wrenching plea into empty space, curiosity gets the better of him and he says, "I apologize for this stupid question, but surely you've noticed there's never a woman sitting on that last stool. Why do you keep on asking out empty space?"

The physicist replies, "Well, according to quantum physics, empty space is never truly empty. Virtual particles come into existence and vanish all the time. You never know when the proper wave function will collapse exactly the right configuration of particles, and the perfect woman might suddenly appear there."

The bartender raises his eyebrows. "Really? Interesting. But couldn't you just ask one of the girls who comes here every Friday if you could buy her a drink? Never know… she might say yes."

The physicist laughs. "Yeah, right —how likely is that to happen?"

A science student out for a walk sees a frog at the side of the road.

"Help!" says the frog, "a wicked witch turned me into a frog! Kiss me to turn me back into a beautiful princess, and we'll marry and live happily ever after."

The nerd picks up the frog, puts it in his pocket, and walks on. The frog sticks its head out and says, "Aren't you going to kiss me?"

"Look," he replies, "I'm a nerd, I don't have room for a girlfriend in my life. But having a talking frog —now that's really neat."

W hy are quantum physicists so confused by sex?

—Because when they find the position, they can't find the momentum, and when they have the momentum, they can't find the position.

A frog went to visit a fortune teller. "What do you see in my future?" asked the frog.

"Very soon," replied the fortune teller, "you will meet a pretty young girl who will want to know everything about you."

"That's great!" said the frog, hopping up and down excitedly. "But when will I meet her?"

"Next week in science class," said the fortune teller.

It Takes Alkynes to Make a World

A man in a hot air balloon realized he was lost. He reduced altitude and spotted a woman below. He descended a bit more and shouted, "Excuse me, can you help me? I promised a friend I would meet him an hour ago, but I don't know where I am."

The woman below replied, "You're in a hot air balloon hovering approximately 30 feet above the ground. You're between 40 and 41 degrees north latitude and between 59 and 60 degrees west longitude."

"You must be an engineer," said the balloonist.

"I am," replied the woman, "But how did you figure that out?"

"Well," answered the balloonist, "everything you told me is technically correct, but I've no idea what to make of your information, and the fact is I'm still lost. Frankly, you've not been much help at all. If anything, you've delayed my trip."

The woman below responded, "You must be in management."

"True," replied the balloonist. "So how did you know?"

"Well," said the woman, "you don't know where you are or where you're going. You have risen to where you are due to a large quantity of hot air. You made a promise which you've no idea how to keep, and you expect people beneath you to solve your problems. The fact is you are in exactly the same position you were in before we met, but now, somehow, it's my fault."

Mr. Perkins, the biology instructor at a posh prep school for young ladies, asked during class, "Miss Smythe, would you please name the organ of the human body which, under appropriate conditions, expands to six times its normal size, and define those conditions."

Miss Smythe gasped, then said icily, "Mr. Perkins, I don't think that is a proper question to ask me. I assure you my parents shall hear of this."

With that, she sat down red-faced. Unperturbed, Mr. Perkins called on Miss Johnson and asked the same question. Miss Johnson, with composure, replied, "The pupil of the eye, in dim light."

"Correct," said Mr. Perkins. "And now, Miss Smythe, I have three things to say to you.

One, you have not studied your lesson.

Two, you have a dirty mind.

And three, you will some day be faced with a dreadful disappointment."

Said another sweet young lady at this same posh school, "Oh, I see how astronomers figure out the distance of the stars and their sizes and temperatures and all that. What really gets me is how they find out what their names are."

And God Said

$$\oiint_{\partial V} \vec{E} \cdot d\vec{A} = \frac{Q}{\epsilon_0}$$

$$\oiint_{\partial V} \vec{B} \cdot d\vec{A} = 0$$

$$\oint_{\partial S} \vec{E} \cdot d\vec{l} = -\iint_S \frac{\partial \vec{B}}{\partial t} \cdot d\vec{A}$$

$$\oint_{\partial S} \vec{B} \cdot d\vec{l} = \mu_0 I_S + \mu_0 \epsilon_0 \iint_S \frac{\partial \vec{E}}{\partial t} \cdot d\vec{A}$$

and *then* there was light.

THE BIG FREAK-OUT IN A PUPPY'S LIFE

Mark Parisi

A brilliant high school chemistry student takes a test, gets his score back, and is dismayed to find that he missed exactly one question. He is especially upset because the question he missed was "how many valence electrons does a hydrogen atom have?" In his haste to complete the test, he had answered 2.

Depressed and despairing, afraid this could affect his chances of getting into MIT, he takes a walk alone along the beach, and is lost in thought when he trips on a metal object in the sand. Picking it up, he finds it to be a brass oil lamp, and as his fingers brush the surface a genie suddenly appears.

The genie thunders, "I can grant you any one wish, but you must answer now. What do you desire?"

The student immediately replies, "I wish I had gotten that question right."

And the universe explodes.

Our young Willie studied chemistry
But Willie is no more
What he took for H_2O
Was really H_2SO_4

Two chemists walk into a restaurant,. The first says "I'll have an H_2O."
The second says "I'll have an H_2O too."
He dies.

Two chemists walk into a restaurant. The first one says, "I'll have an H_2O."

The second one says, "I'll also have a glass of water. But why are you referring to it so formally? We're not at work anymore."

The first chemist goes into the bathroom and cries. His murder plot has been foiled.

A man was peddling books on scientific agriculture. He was having an especially hard time persuading one old farmer. "What do I want them things for?" asked the old farmer.

The peddler answered, "If you had those books, you could farm twice as good as you do now."

The old farmer just laughed. "Hell's bells, son," he said to the peddler, " I already don't farm half as good as I know how to."

A scientist and his wife are out for a drive in the country. They pass by a pasture where a flock of sheep are grazing. The wife says, "Oh look, those sheep have been shorn."

"Yes," says the scientist. "On this side."

It Takes Alkynes to Make a World

Once upon a time there lived three men: a chemist, a physicist, and an engineer. All three had offended the king and were brought to the guillotine to meet their bloody fate. The chemist was led up the stairs first. As he strapped him to the guillotine, the executioner asked, "Head up or head down?"

"Head up," said the chemist.

"Blindfold or no blindfold?"

"No blindfold."

So the executioner swung his axe, cut the rope, and —ZING!— down came the blade. But it stopped barely an inch above the chemist's neck.

Well, the law stated that if an execution didn't succeed the first time, the prisoner had to be released, so the chemist was set free.

Next the physicist was led up to the guillotine. "Head up or head down?" said the executioner.

"Head up," said the physicist.

"Blindfold or no blindfold?"

"No blindfold."

So the executioner swung his axe, cut the rope, and —ZING!— down came the blade. Again it stopped an inch above the would-be victim's neck. Same law, same result. The physicist was also set free.

Finally the engineer was led up to the guillotine. "Head up or head down?" asked the executioner.

"Head up."

"Blindfold or no blindfold?"

"No blindfold."

So the executioner raised his axe, but before he could cut the rope, the engineer yelled out, "Wait!! I see what the problem is!!!"

An optimist sees a glass half-full. A pessimist sees it half-empty.

An engineer sees it twice as large as it needs to be.

Four engineers are hanging out in a bar, knocking down a few brewskis. After a few pints, one of them —no doubt proud of his profession—loudly proclaims that God must be an engineer. This brings hearty cheers from his three companions, and they drink a toast to their fellow professional: God the Engineer.

After another drink, however, matters become a bit more contentious. The original speaker, who happens to be a chemical engineer, now decides to proclaim loudly that God is not just an engineer but, to be precise, a chemical engineer.

"Just look at the human body," he explains. "The blood. The digestive system. All the organs. The living cell itself. A chemical masterpiece!"

Instead of hearty cheers, he is immediately interrupted by one of his chums, the mechanical engineer. "God was clearly a mechanical engineer," he counters. "Just study the bones, the tendons, the ligaments. The smooth functioning of a joint. The articulation of the body in motion. Watch an Olympic athlete and you'll see that God has created the most sublime machine imaginable."

He too is denied any cheering as this time the electrical engineer jumps into the fray. "All that's nothing compared to the human nervous system. The spine and the brain and a thousand miles of ganglia and nerve endings. No computer will ever do everything the human nervous system does. No, I'm afraid, gentlemen, that God is most decidedly an electrical engineer."

But it is the civil engineer who gets the last word. He takes one more chug of beer before offering his proof positive. "God's a civil engineer pure and simple. Who else would have put a major recreational area right next door to the central waste disposal site?"

And that shut them up.

Hilary Price

CARTOON LAWS OF PHYSICS

*"A*nimation follows the laws of physics —
unless it is funnier otherwise."
—Art Babbitt

"I know that this defies the law of gravity,
but, you see, I never studied law."
—Bugs Bunny

1. A body suspended in space will remain in space until made aware of its situation.

2. A body passing through solid matter will leave a hole perfectly conforming to its outline.

3. The time required for an object to fall twenty stories is greater than or equal to the time it takes for whoever knocked it off the ledge to spiral down twenty flights to attempt to capture it unbroken.

4. Certain bodies can pass through solid walls painted to look like tunnel entrances; others cannot.

5. Any violent rearrangement of feline matter is temporary.

6. All inflated balloons are lighter than air and can support whatever weight is tied to their string.

7. Explosive weapons cannot cause fatal injuries.

8. Gravity is transmitted by large, slow-moving waves.

9. Large objects may mysteriously appear when a character reaches behind its back.

10. Holes can be physically picked up and moved.

Derived from the original scientific research of Mark O'Donnell

It Takes Alkynes to Make a World

ASTRONOMER #1: So anyway, this cop pulls me over and asks if I realized that I had just run a red light. So I said that I did not see the light as being red, because it must have blue-shifted as I was approaching it.

ASTRONOMER #2: And he let you go?

ASTRONOMER #1: No. He gave me a speeding ticket instead.

The astronomer was concluding his lecture at the synagogue. "And so the probability is that our own sun will probably die out within the next four or five billion years."

"How many years did you say?" asked Mrs. Siegel from the back of the room.

"Four or five billion," replied the scientist.

"Phew!" said Mrs. Siegel. "I thought you said million."

I have a new theory on inertia but it doesn't seem to be gaining much momentum.

If H_2O is the formula for water, what is the formula for ice?
—$(H_2O)^3$

What is the fastest way to determine the sex of a chromosome?
—Pull down its genes.

Did you hear that Magnesium and Oxygen went on a date?
—OMg!

I was reading a book on anti-gravity. I found it difficult to put down.

Gravity: Not just a good idea. It's the law.

"The only reason for time is so that everything doesn't happen at once."
—Albert Einstein

Particle physics gives me a hadron.

Sodium sodium sodium sodium sodium sodium sodium sodium sodium Batman!

There once was an X from place B,
  That satisfied predicate C.
    He or she did A
    In an adjective way,
  Which resulted in circumstance P.

A friend who's in liquor production,
  Has a still of astounding construction,
    The alcohol boils,
    Through old magnet coils.
  He says that it's proof by induction.

"For a while I lived in Vermont in a house that ran on static electricity. If we wanted to cook something, we had to take a sweater off real quick."
—Steven Wright

Roses are gray.
Violets are gray.
I'm a dog.

Did you hear about that new restaurant on the moon?
—The food's great but there's no atmosphere.

The definition of irony: asking God to help you on a science exam.

Does a radioactive cat have 18 half-lives?

Why do archaeologists drink so much?
—Because their lives are in ruins.

Archaeologists will date anything!

The definition of an archaeologist: One crackpot digging up another cracked pot.

All archaeological research is groundbreaking.

"I was wrong. The sun is not at the center," exclaimed Galileo.

• "I wonder why uranium is fluorescent," said Marie curiously.

• "We had trouble with the propulsion systems for those moon flights," said the NASA engineer apologetically.

• "These genes are dominant," said Tom expressively.

• "The pH of this solution is just 3.5," said Tom half-assedly.

• "I plan to start a cattle ranch in a space station orbiting Jupiter," said Tom jovially.

• "Eating uranium makes me feel funny," said Tom radiantly.

• "I'd risk my life to find out how many electrons that atom is sharing," said Tom valiantly.

• "Those Europeans have a crappy particle accelerator," said Tom discerningly.

• "Dolphin intelligence can save our planet," said Tom superficially.

• "I'm just a self-taught doctor," Tom quacked.

How many pre-meds does it take to screw in a lightbulb?
—Three. One to stand on a stool and screw it in and two to kick the stool out from under him.

• How many archaeologists does it take to change a light bulb?
—Are you kidding?! Why would we want to do that?! The broken bulb is a national treasure, pointing to our rich history and culture.

• How many quantum physicists does it take to screw in a lightbulb?
—One. Two to do it, and one to re-normalise the wave function.

• One.
— How many time-travelers does it take to screw in a lightbulb?

• How many theoretical physicists specializing in general relativity does it take to screw in a lightbulb?
—Two. One to hold the bulb and one to rotate the universe.

• How many astronomers does it take to screw in a lightbulb?
—None. Astronomers prefer the dark.

• How many physicists does it take to screw in a lightbulb?
—If the lightbulb is a perfect sphere, one. The solution for a lightbulb of arbitrary shape is left as an exercise for the reader.

• How many nuclear engineers does it take to screw in a lightbulb?
—Seven. One to screw in the new bulb, and six to figure out what to do with the old one for the next 10,000 years.

• How many lab mice does it take to screw in a lightbulb?
—Two.

Chapter Ten

Brave New World

The Future Ain't What It Used to Be

Andy Singer

*"When we used to listen to the radio,
what were we looking at?"*

Frank Modell

"Progress may have been all right once, but it went on too long."
—Ogden Nash

"The future ain't what it used to be."
—Yogi Berra

"Nostalgia isn't what it used to be."
—Peter De Vries

"My father hated radio and could not wait for television to be invented so he could hate that too."
—Peter De Vries

A robot walks into a bar and orders a drink. The bartender says "Sorry, we don't serve robots."
The robot replies, "You will."

The internet is a lot like ancient Egypt: people write on walls and worship cats.

"So, by a vote of 8 to 2 we have decided to skip the industrial revolution completely, and go right into the electronic age."

Sidney Harris

Two boys are debating about what the greatest invention in the world is. Sammy says "the greatest invention in the world is the lightbulb. You can turn it on and stay awake all night."

But Jimmy disagrees. "No way," he says, "the greatest invention in the world is the automobile. You can get in it and go wherever you want whenever you want."

Neither will admit the other is right, so they go to the town philosopher, Old Man Johnson, who knows a thing or two about a thing or two. Perhaps he can resolve their conflict. Surely he'll be able to tell them what the greatest invention in the world is.

They find the old man on his front porch, looking mighty comfotable in his rocking chair. When they ask him, he just keeps rocking for a while, cogitating hard. Finally he replies: "The thermos has gots to be the best invention of all time because it keeps hot things hot and cold things cold."

Sammy and Jimmy just look at each other, more than a little skeptical. Finally Jimmy challenges the old philosopher: "Yeah, and what's so great about that?"

Old Man Johnson answers, "How do it know?"

"The future always arrives too fast... and in the wrong order."
—Alvin Toffler

"To invent, you need a good imagination and a pile of junk."
—Thomas Edison

"He was a bold man that first ate an oyster."
—Jonathan Swift

"If I had asked people what they wanted, they would have said faster horses."
—Henry Ford

"The wireless telegraph is not difficult to understand. The ordinary telegraph is like a very long cat. You pull the tail in New York, and it meows in Los Angeles. The wireless is the same, only without the cat."
—Albert Einstein

"If GM had kept up with technology like the computer industry has, we would all be driving $25 cars that got 1,000 miles per gallon." —Bill Gates

—Yes, and if cars were like software, they would crash twice a day for no reason, and when you called for service, they'd tell you to reinstall the engine.

CALL ME A FOOLISH VISIONARY, BUT I THINK IT MIGHT JUST BE POSSIBLE TO SQUEEZE THESE THINGS THIN ENOUGH TO FORM A SOFT, FLEXIBLE SHEET WITH WHICH ONE COULD COMFORTABLY BLOW ONE'S NOSE...

Dan Piraro

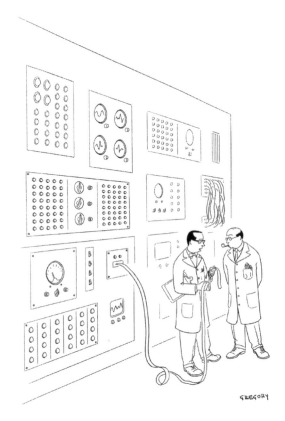

"The results are impressive, but it'll be decades before we can transmit and receive pornography."

Alex Gregory

"I've come up with a set of rules that describe our reactions to technologies:

1. Anything that is in the world when you're born is normal and ordinary and is just a natural part of the way the world works.

2. Anything that's invented between when you're fifteen and thirty-five is new and exciting and revolutionary and you can probably get a career in it.

3. Anything invented after you're thirty-five is against the natural order of things."

—Douglas Adams

Don't anthropomorphize computers. They hate that.

A computer of infinite processing capacity had finally been built and was ready to be put into action. It had been plugged into every data bank, invaded every library, read every book. It had crunched all information to a degree never crunched before.

From all over the world scientists had gathered to be present at its unveiling. Finally, the admin typed in The Big Question:

"Computer, is there a God?"

A tense silence fell over the room as the computer flashed, the screen flickered, and finally the machine responded:

"There is now."

In English, nouns are not masculine or feminine, but they are gender-specific in languages such as French and Spanish, so of course there has been considerable debate in Europe as to how to designate a computer's gender. Is it a he or a she? Predictably, the debate soon became polarized.

The men argued that computers should be referred to in feminine terms because :

• No one but their creator understands their internal logic.
• The native language they use to communicate with other computers is incomprehensible to everyone else.
• Even your smallest mistakes are stored in long-term memory for later retrieval.
• As soon as you make a commitment to one, you find yourself spending half your paycheck on accessories for it.

The women, on the other hand, contended that computers should be referred to as masculine because:

• In order to get their attention, you have to turn them on.
• They are supposed to help you solve problems, but half the time they are the problem.
• They have a lot of data, but are still clueless.
• As soon as you commit to one, you realize that, if you had only waited a little longer, you could have had a better model.

Speech bubbles in comic: "Haha! Where'd you get those old phones?!" / "Do they do anything other than make calls?" / "KIRK AND SPOCK TRAVEL BACK IN TIME TO 2014"

Dan Piraro

Barack Obama, Vladimir Putin, and Bill Gates were summoned by God, who informed them in no uncertain terms that He was very unhappy about the state of affairs on Earth. Since things were so bad, He told the three of them that He was terminating the planet at the end of the week. They were all allowed to return to their homes and businesses and tell their friends and colleagues what was happening, but no matter what they did, God made it clear He was NOT changing His mind.

Barack Obama went in and told his cabinet, "I have good news and I have bad news for you. First the good news: there *is* a God. The bad news is that He is destroying the Earth at the end of the week."

Vladimir Putin went back and told his Politboro 2.0, "I have bad news and I have terrible news. The first is that God speaks English. The second is that He is destroying the Earth at the end of the week."

Bill Gates went back and told his board of directors, "I have good news and I have great news. First, God thinks I am one of the three most important people in the world. Second, you don't have to fix the bugs in Windows 10."

There are four engineers travelling in a car: a mechanical engineer, a chemical engineer, an electrical engineer and a computer engineer. The car breaks down.

"Sounds to me as if the pistons have seized. We'll have to strip down the engine before we can get the car working again," says the mechanical engineer.

"Well," says the chemical engineer, "it sounds to me as if the fuel might be contaminated. I think we should purge the fuel system."

"I'm betting it's a timing problem," says the electrical engineer, "or maybe a faulty plug lead."

They all turn to the computer engineer, who has said nothing, and ask, "Well, what do you think?"

"Ummm —I think we should all just get out of the car and then get back in."

There are 10 kinds of people in this world: those who understand binary, and those who don't.

"On the Internet, nobody knows you're a dog."

Peter Steiner

"Damn webcam! Now *everyone* knows
I'm a dog!"

© MARK ANDERSON, WWW.ANDERTOONS.COM

Mark Anderson

"We loved Tuscany. The cell reception was fantastic and the Wi-Fi was to die for."

Robert Mankoff

What's the difference between going to jail and installing a new Microsoft product on your computer?
—When you go to jail you get one free phone call.

If Bill Gates had a nickel for every time *Windows* crashed... oh, wait a sec, *he does*.

If at first you don't succeed, call it version 1.0.

"I realized my little nephew will never know life without *Facebook*. He'll never know what it's like to go, 'I wonder what happened to that guy Chris from high school?' and then just shrug his shoulders and move on. "
— Ophira Eisenberg

Dan Piraro

Dist. by King Features BIZARRO.COM

"Computers are useless. They can only give you answers."
—Pablo Picasso

The programmer's wife tells him, "Run to the store and pick up a loaf of bread. If they have eggs, get a dozen."

The programmer comes home with 12 loaves of bread.

How many geeks does it take to ruin a joke?
—Wait. First of all, it's nerds, not geeks. And it's a riddle, not a joke. Now go ahead...

My brain has too many tabs open.

"I'm also available in .pdf format if you're more comfortable with that."

Christopher Burke

"Hello...technical support?"

David Sipress

Computer Nerd: A guy who knows 147 technically possible ways to have sex but doesn't know any women.

A man received the following e-mail from his neighbor:

Subject: Confession

I am so sorry, Bob. I've been riddled with guilt and I have to confess. I have been tapping your wife, day and night, when you're not around. In fact, more than you. I'm not getting any at home, but that's no excuse. I can no longer live with the guilt and I hope you will accept my sincerest apology with my promise that it won't happen again.

The husband, anguished and betrayed, went into his bedroom, grabbed his gun and, without a word, shot his wife and killed her.

A few moments later, a second e-mail came in:

Damn autocorrect. I meant "wifi", not "wife."

How do you know when a computer nerd is flirting with you?

—He stares at *your* shoes.

The head of a start-up tech company was surprised one day by a Labor Department audit.

"Does everyone here make at least the minimum wage?"

"Oh, yes," said the entrepreneur, "except the half-wit."

"Oh?" snapped the inspector. "And what does the half-wit earn?"

"Let's see," said the owner. "I'd say it works out to about two bucks an hour, plus all the cold coffee he can drink, and a stale fruitcake at Christmas."

"Well," said the government man, "you just go bring this so-called half-wit in here right now so I can question him."

"Don't have to," said the entrepreneur. "You're already talking to him."

Why was the programmer stuck in the shower?
—She was just following instructions: "Lather. Rinse. Repeat."

If you want to understand recursion, you need to understand recursion first.

So this hacker walks into a bar and keeps making demand after demand after demand of the server...

There's a band called 1023 MB. They haven't had any gigs yet.

"Computers have been taught to recognize music, create melodies and harmonies, and actually compose tunes. Once they learn to trash hotels and show up late for concerts, they'll be all set."
—Jay Leno

What's the biggest lie in the entire universe?
"I have read and agree to the Terms of Service."
SECOND BIGGEST LIE: By clicking I agree I am at least 18 years of age.

"Remember, they're Trekkies, so try to work in the space-time continuum."

© MARK ANDERSON, WWW.ANDERTOONS.COM

Mark Anderson

It was a sweltering August day in 1946 when the four Cohen brothers entered the posh Dearborn, Michigan, offices of Henry Ford, the car maker. "Mr. Ford," announced Norman Cohen, the eldest of the four, "we have a remarkable invention that will revolutionize the car industry: automobile air conditioning."

Ford looked skeptical, but their threat to offer it to the competition kept his interest piqued. "We would like to demonstrate it to you in person." They brought Mr. Ford outside and asked him to enter a black automobile parked in front of the building.

Hiram Cohen, the second brother, opened the door of the car. "Please step inside, Mr. Ford."

Ford got in and immediately exclaimed, "My God, it feels like two hundred degrees in here!"

"Not for long," smiled the third brother, Max. "Just push the white button." Ford pushed the button and all of a sudden a whoosh of freezing air started blowing from vents all around the car, and within seconds the automobile was not only comfortable, it was quite cool.

The old man got very excited and invited them back to the office, where he asked them how much they wanted for the patent.

Lowell, the fourth brother, spoke up, "The price is only one million dollars, but there is a condition: The name *Cohen Brothers Air-Conditioning* must be stamped right next to the Ford logo on every vehicle using our invention."

"Money is no problem," retorted Ford, "but no way will I allow a Jewish name next to *my* logo on *my* cars!"

They haggled back and forth for a couple of hours, but finally they settled: Five million dollars, but the name *Cohen* would be left off. However, the first names of the Cohen brothers would be forever emblazoned upon the console of every Ford air conditioning system.

And that is why, to this day, whenever you enter a Ford vehicle, you will see those four names clearly printed on the air conditioning control panel:
LO, NORM, HI and *MAX*.

Technology advances; people stay the same.

Leigh Rubin

I only had enough room to go up to 2012.

Ha! That'll freak somebody out someday.

Dan Piraro

"Never make predictions, especially about the future."
—Casey Stengel

"Wall Street indices predicted nine out of the last five recessions."
—Paul A. Samuelson

"An economist is an expert who will know tomorrow why the things he predicted yesterday didn't happen today."
—Evan Esar

"I have seen the future and it is very much like the present, only longer."
—Kehlog Albran

"I was a peripheral visionary. I could see the future, but only way off to the side."
—Steven Wright

The future just happened.

How does a man show that he is planning for the future?
—He buys two cases of beer.

Did you hear about last night's futurists meeting?
—It got cancelled due to unforeseen circumstances.

I nearly fell in love with a futurist, but he left me before we met.

If the Mayans were any good at predicting the future then there would still be Mayans.

"Well folks, it is December 21, or as the Mayans call it, *April Fools Day*."
—Jay Leno

Dear Internet People of 2012:

This is Maya

This is Aztec

And this is Oreo

Calvin and Hobbes

A NEW DECADE IS COMING UP.

YEAH, BIG DEAL! HMPH.

WHERE ARE THE FLYING CARS? WHERE ARE THE MOON COLONIES? WHERE ARE THE PERSONAL ROBOTS AND THE ZERO GRAVITY BOOTS, HUH? YOU CALL THIS A NEW DECADE?! YOU CALL THIS THE FUTURE?? HA!

WHERE ARE THE ROCKET PACKS? WHERE ARE THE DISINTEGRATION RAYS? WHERE ARE THE FLOATING CITIES?

FRANKLY, I'M NOT SURE PEOPLE HAVE THE BRAINS TO MANAGE THE TECHNOLOGY THEY'VE GOT.

I MEAN· LOOK AT THIS! WE STILL HAVE WEATHER?! GIVE ME A BREAK!

CALVIN AND HOBBES © 1989 Watterson. Reprinted with permission of UNIVERSAL UCLICK. All rights reserved.

Bill Watterson

"And now The Mayan Channel weather forecast.
THURSDAY: cloudy, chance of showers, high 39.
FRIDAY: volcanoes, asteroid strikes, apocalypse."
—David Letterman

"It's late Friday night, which means the world did not end after all! So the good news is, we're still here. The bad news: I got a lot of Christmas shopping to do."
—Jimmy Fallon

"Don't worry about the world coming to an end today. It's already tomorrow in Australia."
—Charles M. Schulz

"If the world comes to an end, I want to be in Cincinnati. Everything comes there ten years later."
—Mark Twain

"The groundhog is like most other prophets; it delivers its prediction and then disappears."
—Bill Vaughan

A Cherokee elder is asked by members of his tribe, "Will it be cold this winter?" Not wanting to appear ignorant, he tells them, "Yes, it will be cold this winter. I suggest you start collecting firewood."

The tribe disperses immediately to start gathering wood. Out of sight, the elder heads to a phone and calls the National Weather Service. He asks, "Will it be cold this winter?" The agent at the NWS responds, "Yes, our early data indicates that it will be a cold winter."

The elder returns to the tribe and tells them, "Keep collecting wood! A cold winter is on the way!" A few days later, just to be sure, he calls the NWS, and again he asks, "Will it be cold this winter?" The agent responds, "Our data now suggests that the winter will be very cold."

The elder informs his tribe, "It will be a very cold winter! More wood! More wood!" Days pass and so much hard work is being done gathering the wood that the chief wants to be 100% certain. He calls the NWS one last time. "Are you absolutely positive that it will be very cold this winter?"

"Absolutely!" says the NWS agent. "The Cherokee are collecting firewood like crazy."

PREDICTING THE FUTURE

1486: "So many centuries after the Creation it is unlikely that anyone could find hitherto unknown lands of any value." —Advisors to King Ferdinand and Queen Isabella

1800: "What, sir, would you make a ship sail against the wind and currents by lighting a bonfire under her deck? I pray you, excuse me, I have not the time to listen to such nonsense." —Napoleon Bonaparte, when told of Robert Fulton's steamboat

1828: "Rail travel at high speed is not possible because passengers, unable to breathe, would die of asphyxia." —Dr. Dionysus Larder

1869: "I see no good reasons why the views given in this volume should shock the religious sensibilities of anyone."
—Charles Darwin, *The Origin Of Species*

1872: "It's a great invention but who would want to use it anyway?"
—President Rutherford B. Hayes, after a demonstration of Alexander Bell's telephone

1873: "The abdomen, the chest, and the brain will forever be shut from the intrusion of the wise and humane surgeon."
—Sir John Eric Ericksen, Surgeon-Extraordinary to Queen Victoria

1876: "This 'telephone' has too many shortcomings to be seriously considered as a means of communication. The device is inherently of no value to us."
—Western Union internal memo

1889: "Fooling around with alternating current is just a waste of time. Nobody will use it, ever." —Thomas Edison

1899: "Everything that can be invented has been invented." —Charles H. Duell, Commissioner, U.S. Office of Patents

1907: "To-day, in the City of New York, sixty-six different tongues are spoken. A century hence, there will probably be one."
—*The American Historical Magazine*

1912: "The coming of the wireless era will make war impossible, because it will make war ridiculous." —Guglielmo Marconi

1920s: "The wireless music box has no imaginable commercial value. Who would pay for a message sent to nobody in particular?" —David Sarnoff's associates arguing against his recommendation for investment in the radio.

1920: "A rocket will never be able to leave the Earth's atmosphere." —*NY Times;* officially retracted on July 17, 1969, as Apollo 11 was on its way to the moon.

1921: "Professor Goddard does not know the relation between action and reaction and the need to have something better than a vacuum against which to react. He seems to lack the basic knowledge ladled out daily in high schools." —*NY Times* editorial about Goddard's revolutionary rocket work

1923: "There is no likelihood man can ever tap the power of the atom."
—Robert Millikan (Nobel Prize in Physics)

1927: "Who the hell wants to hear actors talk?" —H. M. Warner, Warner Brothers

1932: "There is not the slightest indication that nuclear energy will ever be obtainable. It would mean that the atom would have to be shattered at will." —Albert Einstein

1946: "Television won't last because people will soon get tired of staring at a plywood box every night." —Darryl Zanuck

1949: "Computers in the future may weigh no more than 1.5 tons." —*Popular Mechanics*

1957: "Space travel is bunk." —Sir Harold Spencer Jones, Astronomer Royal

1957: "I have traveled the length and breadth of this country and talked with the best people, and I can assure you that data processing is a fad that won't last out the year." —An editor in charge of business books for Prentice Hall

1962: "Transmission of documents via telephone wires is possible in principle, but the apparatus required is so expensive that it will never become a practical proposition." —Dennis Gabor

1968: "But what ... is it good for?" —IBM Engineer commenting on the microchip

1969: "We can close the books on infectious diseases."
—U.S. Surgeon-General William H. Stewart

1977: "There is no reason anyone would want a computer in their home."
—Ken Olson, president of Digital Equipment Corp

FROM "OKLAHOMA"

LYRICS BY OSCAR HAMMERSTEIN

Everything's up to date in Kansas City
They've gone about as fer as they can go
They went an' built a skyscraper seven stories high
About as high as a buildin' orta grow.
Everything's like a dream in Kansas City
It's better than a magic lantern show.
You can turn the radiator on whenever you want some heat
With every kind of comfort every house is all complete.
You can walk to privies in the rain and never wet your feet
They've gone about as fer as they can go.
They've gone about as fer as they can go!

Mark Parisi

211

"Boys, Colonel Mustard did this in the library with a Kindle."

Graham Sale

When the inventor of the drawing board messed things up, what exactly did he go back to?

Do you reckon Thomas Edison got one of those lightbulb-above-the-head moments and thought, "Damn it, I'm going to make me one of those things!"

My husband's totally into DIY. He just built a set of shelves for our den and now he's writing some books to put on them.

I wonder if the guy who invented the airbag spent a lot of time thinking about it or if it just popped into his head.

Hundreds of years ago a scientist came up to me and asked me what I thought of ink, his new invention. I said the idea looked good on paper.

The guy who invented applause must have looked like an idiot when he first tried it out.

Although my father and I worked together inventing the first rear-view mirror, we're not as close as we appear.

I've just invented a new word: "Plagiarism"

Brave New World

I changed all my passwords to "incorrect" so whenever I forget, it says "Your password is incorrect."

W hat do programmers and cats have in common?
—When either one is unusually excited, an appropriate question is, "Did you find a bug?"

A UNIX saleslady, Lenore,
   Enjoys work, but she likes the
      beach more.
      She found a good way
      To combine work and play:
   She sells C shells by the seashore.

"I t's a unit of electric current," said Tom amply.

• "This is the most common language used on micros," said Tom basically.

• "languages computer forget don't," said Tom forthwith.

• "I have to fix all the bugs and add some new features," Tom maintained.

• "Someone stole my electrolytic capacitor!" Tom charged negatively.

• "But I don't know C++," Tom objected.

• "I'd better repeat that SOS signal. No one seems to have heard us," said Tom remorsefully.

• "Goodbye, and thanks for the long-distance radio. Now it'll be easier to stay in touch," said Tom with a short wave.

• "Let's invest in a high-tech startup!" Tom ventured.

• "That laser beam sure took care of MIT!" the mad scientist cackled in Zapotec.

Isabella Bannerman

US006826983B1

(12) **United States Patent**
Magdi

(10) **Patent No.:** **US 6,826,983 B1**
(45) **Date of Patent:** **Dec. 7, 2004**

LIGHT BULB CHANGER

(75) Inventor: **Thomas Magdi**, 888 Hamilton Ave., Rockledge, FL (US) 32955

(73) Assignee: **Thomas Magdi**, Rockledge, FL (US)

(*) Notice: Subject to any disclaimer, the term of this patent is extended or adjusted under 35 U.S.C. 154(b) by 0 days.

(21) Appl. No.: **10/361,528**

(22) Filed: **Feb. 10, 2003**

ABSTRACT

A light bulb changer method and apparatus that contains components that allows for instantly detecting a burned out light, automatically removing the burned out light, and automatically replacing the burned out light with a replacement bulb. The changer operates without human intervention, and can be assembled from a kit having a light fixture, detecting sensor, removing and replacement hardware. The kit can allow a consumer to assemble the changer for use as a novelty item, and/or also to be used as a working light fixture, such as a table lamp, and the like. The changer can also be used as a retrofit for existing light fixtures so that the existing light fixtures can be modified.

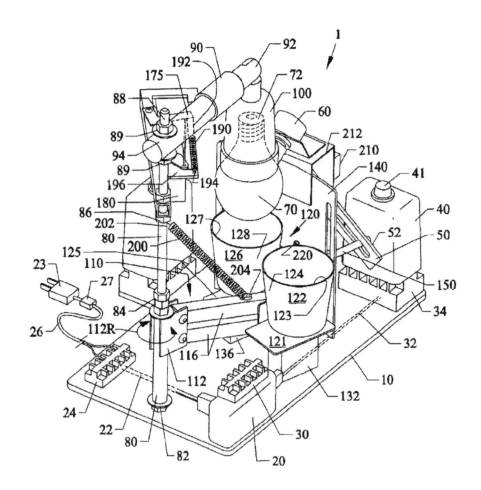

How many programmers does it take to screw in a lightbulb?
—That's hardware.

• How many tech-support staff does it take to screw in a lightbulb?
—We have a lightbulb here, and it works fine. Can you tell me what kind of bulb you have? Okay. There could be four or five things wrong. Now, have you turned the light switch off and on?

• How many computer salesmen does it take to screw in a lightbulb?
—I'll get back to you.

• How many Microsoft engineers does it take to screw in a lightbulb?
—None. They'll simply define darkness as a new standard.

• How many web designers does it take to screw in a lightbulb?
— Not applicable. They always leave right before the problems start.

• How many oracles does in take to screw in a lightbulb?
—No one knows. LED bulbs outlive oracles.

• How many inventors does it take to screw in a lightbulb?
—Your NDA or mine?

• How many futurists does in take to screw in a lightbulb?
—Sorry, but you'll have to wait for the sequel...

Bradford Veley

Cartoonist Index

Flake, Emily
pp. 24, 145
© Emily Flake / The New Yorker Collection / The Cartoon Bank
www.emilyflake.com

Gerberg, Mort
p. 89
© Mort Gerberg / The New Yorker Collection / The Cartoon Bank
www.mortgerberg.com

Goddard, Clive
p. 185
© Clive Goddard, with permission of Cartoonstock.com
www.clivegoddard.com

Gregory, Alex
p. 200
© Alex Gregory/ The New Yorker Collection / The Cartoon Bank

Gumpertz, Robert
p. 56
© Robert Gumpertz
www.gumpertzart.com

Hamilton, Willliam
p. 90
© William Hamilton / The New Yorker Collection / The Cartoon Bank

Handelsman, JB
p. 34
© JB Handelsman / The New Yorker Collection / The Cartoon Bank

Hanley
p. 181
© The New Yorker Collection / The Cartoon Bank

Harris, Sidney
pp. 40, 41, 42, 58, 64, 74, 140, 176, 198
© Sidney Harris; with permission of Cartoonstock.com
www.sciencecartoonsplus.com

Hickerson, Buddy
pp. 111, 179
© Buddy Hickerson
www.creators.com/comics/the-quigmans-about.html

Hilburn, Scott
p. 14
© 2010 Scott Hilburn. Dist. By Universal Uclick. Reprinted with permission. All rights reserved.
www.theargylesweater.com

Hixson, Vivian
pp. 35, 36, 50, 52
© Vivian S. Hixson

Hobbs, Jeff
pp. 73, 183
© Jeff Hobbs
jeffmhobbs.wix.com/cartoons

Hokinson, Helen E.
p. 140
© Helen E. Hokinson/ The New Yorker Collection / The Cartoon Bank

Johnson, Carolita
p. 79
© Carolita Johnson / The New Yorker Collection / The Cartoon Bank
carolitajohnson.squarespace.com

Kanin, Zach
pp. 23, 25, 186
© Zach Kanin / The New Yorker Collection / The Cartoon Bank

Kopf, L.J.
pp. 55, 142
© L.J. Kopf

Kovarsky, Anatol
p. 112
© Anatol Kovarsky / The New Yorker Collection / The Cartoon Bank

Leighton, Robert
pp. 83, 163
© Robert Leighton / The New Yorker Collection / The Cartoon Bank
www.robert-leighton.com

Lewis, Eric
p. 163
© Eric Lewis / The New Yorker Collection / The Cartoon Bank
www.ericlewis.com

Schwartz, Benjamin

p. 141
© Benjamin Schwartz / The New Yorker Collection / The Cartoon Bank

Shanahan, Danny

pp. 12, 118, 145
© Danny Shanahan / The New Yorker Collection / The Cartoon Bank
dannyshanahan.com

Singer, Andy

pp. 12, 31, 49, 51, 76, 152, 158, 197
© Andy Singer
www.andysinger.com

Sipress, David

pp. 13, 33, 50, 82, 159, 205
© David Sipress / The New Yorker Collection / The Cartoon Bank

Soderblom, Paul

pp. 9, 67, 128
© Paul Soderblom

Steiner, Peter

p. 202
© Peter Steiner / The New Yorker Collection / The Cartoon Bank
www.plsteiner.com

Stevens, Mick

p. 28, 73
© Mick Stevens / The New Yorker Collection / The Cartoon Bank
www.mickstevens.com

Stevenson, James

p. 92
© James Stevenson / The New Yorker Collection / The Cartoon Bank

Stivers, Mark

pp. 14, 64, 71, 101, 180
© Mark Stivers
www.stiverscartoons.com

Tobey, Barney

p. 75
© Barney Tobey / The New Yorker Collection / The Cartoon Bank

Toos, Andrew

pp. 37, 51, 106
© Andrew Toos; with permission of Cartoonstock.com

Trudeau, G.B.

p. 39
Doonesbury © 1985 G. B. Trudeau. Reprinted with permission of Universal Uclick. All rights reserved.

Veley, Bradford

pp. 41, 47, 74, 81, 98, 149, 168, 180, 187, 215
© Bradford Veley
www.bradveley.com

Walsh, Liam Francis

p. 109
© Liam Francis Walsh / The New Yorker Collection / The Cartoon Bank
liamfranciswalsh.com

Watterson, Bill

pp. 15, 35, 45, 69. 77, 80, 97, 144, 162, 165, 209
Calvin And Hobbes © 1995 Watterson. Reprinted with permission of Universal Uclick. All rights reserved.
www.calvinandhobbes.com

Wilson, Gahan

p. 113
Archival material from Playboy magazine. Copyright © 1967 by Playboy. Reprinted with permission. All rights reserved.
www.gahanwilson.net

Ziegler, Jack

pp. 27, 162, 175
© Jack Ziegler / The New Yorker Collection / The Cartoon Bank

John Towsen

John's most recent book, *Clowns*, came out 39 years ago, so he figured it was high time for another. Yes, he really does have a Ph.D (drama, NYU) —which will no doubt come as a surprise to some of his friends— as well as an NEH fellowship and a Fulbright. He grew up in New York City's Greenwich Village, where he still lives, and had his first exposure to laugh-so-hard-it-hurts comedy when he saw Danny Kaye on the big screen, probably in *The Court Jester* (1955). A few days after his 7th birthday he made his live television debut in a comedy sketch with Red Skelton and Jackie Gleason on *The Red Skelton Show*. He subsequently acted in dozens of television shows and commercials, working alongside such names as Gary Moore, Julie Andrews, Kaye Ballard, Alice Ghostley, Edie Adams, Myrna Loy, Claudette Colbert, Robert Preston, Tab Hunter, Sid Caesar, Ed Wynn, Claude Rains, Charlie Ruggles, Walter Slezak, Kate Smith, Shirley Booth, Sam Levenson, Margaret Hamilton, Patty Duke, and Joseph Papp. In his twenties he returned to show biz, this time somehow eking out a living in the world of clown and physical comedy, from the schools of Long Island to the circus sands of Saskatchewan, Saudi Arabia, and points in between, most of it with partner Fred Yockers. He was artistic director for the first two New York international clown-theatre festivals (1983, 1985) and has taught full-length physical comedy courses at Princeton University, Ohio University, and the Juilliard School, plus innumerable shorter workshops in numerous countries. Former students include Laura Linney, Jeanne Tripplehorn, Andre Braugher, Michael Hayden, and Michael Stuhlbarg. His latest research on physical comedy is to be found on his blog: *physicalcomedy.blogspot.com*. In other parallel lives he taught theatre, multimedia, and digital video in the Creative Arts & Technology program at Bloomfield College for 26 years, and spent many a summer working for the Open Society Institute doing media training for activists in hot spots across the globe.

You see, even 35 years ago he was interested in the interplay between words and image.

Photo: Jim Moore

39959962R00126

Made in the USA
San Bernardino, CA
07 October 2016